MICHAEL OLESKER'S BALTIMORE

Michael Olesker's

BALTIMORE

IF YOU LIVE HERE, YOU'RE HOME

THE JOHNS HOPKINS UNIVERSITY PRESS

BALTIMORE AND LONDON

© 1995 Michael Olesker
All rights reserved. Published 1995
Printed in the United States of America on acid-free paper
04 03 02 01 00 99 98 97 96 95   5 4 3 2 1

The Johns Hopkins University Press
2715 North Charles Street
Baltimore, Maryland 21218-4319
The Johns Hopkins Press Ltd., London

Library of Congress Cataloging-in-Publication Data will be
found at the end of this book.

A catalog record for this book is available from the British Library.

ISBN 0-8018-5203-X

To my family, and to the memory of my father

CONTENTS

ACKNOWLEDGMENTS

Thanks are due to some people in the newspaper business who helped me over the years.

The man who broke me in and became my professional godfather was the sports editor at the *News American*, John Steadman. Without him opening the door for me, and then going to bat when I needed it, I shudder to think what I might do for a living today.

Others at that newspaper, which is now unfortunately a downtown parking lot, gave guidance and a sense of journalistic freedom I will always treasure: Steve O'Neill, Bill Stump, Vida Roberts, Art Janney, Marvin Beard, and the late Tom White and Lou Linley.

At the *Sun*, I've had the good fortune to be surrounded by people generally smarter than I am and generously forgiving of my shortcomings. Among them: Gil Watson, the heart of the paper's newsroom and a man who gives me all the rope I can handle; Tom Linthicum, a steady hand during some difficult seasons; and Jim Keat, John Plunkett, Tony Barbieri, and Paul Banker, who hired me.

Editor John Carroll has made the newsroom a healthy and welcoming place for me. He and managing editor Bill Marimow have been enormously encouraging, no small gift to someone putting his ego on the line three times a week.

Also, there have been colleagues at both the *Sun* and the *News American* from whose intelligence and wit I've gained, and I thank them: Sandy Banisky, Fraser Smith, Mike Ollove, Jonathan Bor, Eileen Canzian, Rafael Alvarez, Peter Jensen, Harold Jackson, Mike Littwin, Mark Hyman, John Robinson, Joe Nawrozki, E. Lee Lassiter, Jim Henneman, Gregory Kane, Antero Pietila, Doug Birch, Alice Steinbach, Pat McGuire, Fred Rasmussen, Jacques Kelly, JoAnn Rodgers, Clem Florio, and Chuck McGeehan. And Mike Forrest, the computer genius at WJZ-TV who found a way past various electronic obstacles to get this book into print.

Thanks, also, to Ron Shapiro, who encouraged me to put this collection together and then had the courage I lacked to approach Hopkins Press; and to Bob Brugger at Hopkins, for his patience and guidance along the way.

And finally, thanks to Suzy, my wife and confidant and unofficial editor.

PROLOGUE

A City Like a Sheepish Teenager

Baltimore is a city of tribal rituals, of neighbors sharing steamed crabs in the back yard, and downtown waitresses who call their customers Hon without worrying about any vast sociological implications, and worshipful football fans who believe the snatching of their beloved Colts was the worst kidnapping since the Lindbergh baby.

It's a town so historically self-conscious of its municipal shortcomings, real and imagined, that it shuns the limelight like some sheepish teenager and hopes no one will notice it in all of its infinite flaws.

But, when it thinks nobody's looking, it can dance a little number to make your heart lilt. It's a place where Queen Elizabeth of England was escorted onto the field at Memorial Stadium one night before an Orioles baseball game. People are respectful enough around here, but not much impressed by royalty. From the upper deck came a fan's good-natured howl: "Take off that hat, Queenie, we can't see dem O's." Apparently unnoticed: the queen happened to be hatless.

The out-of-towners have only vague notions of this city. They've heard about Harborplace, which draws more people than Disney World, and the Orioles, who draw more people than anyone ever imagined, and the idiosyncratic four-time mayor named Schaefer, who became governor and complained in his quiet moments, "My head's too big, and I walk like a duck."

But these are just the famous items. It's a town where people still talk of corner bars and say, "Ah, now there was a saloon . . . "

Like Eddie Bunn's place on Pratt Street, where the legendary John LaVeck showed up one day with a pig on a rope. LaVeck tied the pig to a parking meter and went into the bar, but not before depositing coins in the meter so the pig wouldn't get ticketed.

Or Dolan's on Greenmount Avenue. Those who got a little weary at

Dolan's were invited to rest in the basement. The resting place was a casket, kept for just such occasions.

It's a town where Hunky Sauerhoff gets hundreds of people to join his Loyal Sons of Pigtown, because they think Hunky's a swell piece of work. How swell? Well, he once went to a dog track in Florida and placed a large bet on a dog. The dog trailed badly. Bye-bye, large bet. But then somebody—the police indicate it was Hunky—threw a cat onto the track, scattering the dogs and scratching the whole race.

These are the stories that are told and retold through the years. A city's a place with little unofficial histories, which are written when people spend lives together. In suburbia, there's too much air conditioning, and the yards are too big. Distance prevails. This is fine for nature lovers or hermits, but not for people who like company, who need the give and take of human contact. Out of this comes actual personalities, and not some reflection of a thing seen on a television screen.

Baltimoreans have always been reminded that, collectively, they're a kind of homely stepchild, a wayward schoolkid stuck between the glitter children of New York and Washington. Like a child in any family, or any classroom, you look for your spot. If you're not considered one of the shiny-brights in class, you make your mark when the teacher's got her back turned. You glimpse an opening, you dance your dance, and then you duck back out of the limelight. Some children never quite outgrow such a mentality. Sometimes, it threads its way through the personality of a whole community, which learns to embrace it if it is wise.

Baltimore's always had entire neighborhoods of marginalized people. We tend to settle down in packs, and nurse our insecurities, and simultaneously nurture the things that make us unique. It's true of the Poles and the Italians and the Greeks of East Baltimore, the blacks of West Baltimore, the Jews of Northwest Baltimore. When the entrenched majority makes you feel slightly outcast over long periods of time, you stop trying to mimic the majority and embrace the things handed down to you. This is the Baltimore that I treasure.

I enter the picture with a few vagrant notions rolling around in my head. I identified with that kid who wasn't the brightest fellow in class, but I was also smart enough to spot my opening: There were so many wonderful characters ad-libbing their way through life, so many stories waiting to be told.

My family moved here from the Bronx, not long after World War II. My father, having dropped out his freshman year at New York University to join the war, brought us here so he could finish school on the GI Bill. I was four years old. We lived in the Latrobe housing projects for four years and then, with my father standing by his checkbook and feigning solvency, we moved to Northwest Baltimore.

My memories of home are filled with newspapers lying in all of the rooms. I saw them when I was forced to come home from whatever neighborhood ballgames were in season. When I read the *Sun*, a baseball writer named Lou Hatter made me see that games could be described with wit and grace. When I found a paper then known as the *News-Post*, I saw a columnist named John Steadman writing about the human beings behind the box scores. I was in junior high school when the thought first occurred to me: Maybe there's an opening in that business for a guy like me.

I started writing when I joined my high school newspaper, which was called the *Collegian*. The high school was Baltimore City College. The *Collegian* appeared every Friday of the school year, and everybody on it was a genius, plus me.

I sat at the typewriter every week, pecked out my little story, and then handed it to the paper's managing editor, a fellow named Robert Miller whose IQ was higher than my weight. Every week, he'd read my stuff and look for something nice to say, something marvelously encouraging, to boost my confidence. He always said the same thing: "It's very well typed."

With this rocket thrust of enthusiasm lifting me, I went to the University of Maryland and majored in journalism. There the school paper, called the *Diamondback*, appeared every weekday. Those of us who took it seriously spent most of our nights putting out the paper, and most of our days sleeping. Thus, many of us completed the four-year undergraduate program in what we used to call "the full five years."

In my senior year, I took a course called Advanced Editing, with a professor named Newsom. On the first morning of class, Dr. Newsom said he wouldn't be holding any more classes. Instead, each of us would be assigned to one of the area's professional newspapers—the *Washing-*

ton Post, the *Evening Star* or, in Baltimore, the *Sun* or the *News American.* We'd work on the copy desk, editing stories and writing headlines, and at the end of the semester we'd be graded on how well we'd handled ourselves.

I was assigned the *News American.* The copy chief was a fellow who'll go nameless here, though I owe him a lot. He goes unnamed because I'm about to call him a drunk. For his drinking, which routinely made him senseless by midday, I will always be grateful.

In my first week on the copy desk, I was assigned a dreadful collection of stories to edit, which, in my youthful dementia, I considered beneath my abilities. So I decided, what the hell, I won't go back. Dr. Newsom will never check, and he'll give me a good grade because I'm a senior and he knows me.

So now, months later, it's the last week of school. I'm walking through the journalism building in College Park and bump into Dr. Newsom, who immediately asks, "How are things at the *News American?*"

"Great," I lie.

"Good," he says. "I'll be calling all the copy chiefs. And, based on what they tell me, you'll get your grade."

I saw my entire life pass before me—and, frankly, it wasn't the kind of life I'd had in mind. I had visions of getting kicked out of school and, worse, my parents would holler at me. So I drove immediately to Baltimore, raced up to the third floor of the *News American,* and looked for the copy chief. I saw him slumped on a chair in a corner of the clattery newsroom, eyes at half-mast, in an alcoholic fog.

"Sir," I said, fully prepared to suck up as I had never in my life previously sucked up, "I don't know if you remember me. My name is Michael Olesker. And, uh, I was here 16 weeks ago, at the start of the school semester."

The copy chief looked up at me with glazed eyes then, and took several long seconds to attempt to recognize me.

"I was supposed to come back every week since then," I said humbly.

"Well," he replied, after a moment in which the earth stood still, "you did, didn't you?"

"Yes," I said, knowing an opening when I saw one. "It's been one of the most moving experiences of my life."

"That's good," he said, nodding slowly. "I think you've done excellent work, and if you want, I'll write you a letter of recommendation."

I got an *A* in the course, and the *News American* hired me to be a professional newspaper reporter.

The morning after I graduated college, I started work there and commenced my actual education. I was 22 years old and built like dental floss. An editor named Tom Hughes, who might have been 50 but looked older, spotted me the moment I walked in and knew a mark when he saw one.

"Young man," he said, "do you work here?"

I thought: Oh, no, he's heard that I didn't show up for 16 weeks on the copy desk. I summoned all of my verbal dexterity and boldly declared: "Huh?"

"Because, if you do," said Hughes, leaning his tall, praying mantis of a body in very close, "then I'd better not catch you doing your laundry in the men's room sink."

"No, sir, I . . . "

But he'd already turned on his heels and stalked off. In a little while, a reporter named Harry "Fire Alarm" Riley walked into the newsroom, stood on a desk, and bellowed out the day's train schedules, just because the spirit moved him. He did this routinely. There was a rewrite man, Byron Roberts, who decided to run for mayor. You can't win, everybody told him. I know, said Roberts, but when I die, the obits will all have to say, "Byron Roberts, former candidate for mayor of Baltimore, . . . "

I started sensing a kinship here. It was a bunch of people like me, not quite as bookish as the Ivy League guys up Calvert Street at the *Sun*, but bright enough to spot an opening when it came along. They were like entire neighborhoods of people in this city: feeling a little marginalized, feeling unlike the shiny-brights of Washington and New York, but having a swell time doing their little dance when the spirit moved them.

The managing editor was a fellow named Tom White, who studied the racing forms between editions and then strolled into the sports office, where he'd place his offtrack wagers, tightly wrapped in copy paper, into the hands of a slight, stooped, unassuming clerk named Walter Penkilo, who would then run the bets upstairs to the composing room, where some of the crew ran a profitable gambling operation.

Penkilo worked for John Steadman. Steadman batted out a big-hearted column six days a week while dragging in guys off the street like the racetrack tout Mr. Diz, and Balls Maggio, whose profession was rescuing balls from the Jones Falls basin and thereafter selling them. These guys made no claims to being jet-setters; they were nobody's prize pupils. They were just Baltimore.

One day, on no particular whim, Steadman wore his old Navy uniform to work, wrote his column, then headed upstairs to the composing room to lay out his section's pages. The city editor, Eddie Ballard, got an idea. He sent a reporter named John Jennings outside to grab a friendly cop and tell him there was a fellow up in the composing room who should be arrested for impersonating a military officer.

When the cop came in, all hell broke loose. The guys in the composing room saw his uniform and thought it was a raid on their gambling operation. They bolted for the exits. The cop never arrested Steadman; turned out they were old friends.

In my head, there were notions of one day writing a metro column, a job held in those days by a guy named Seymour Kopf. Seymour was a man given to flights of lunacy, in and out of print. Cornering me in the newsroom one morning, he announced he was getting married. It would be his sixth bride. I asked him what had happened with the first five. They were captured by the communists, he explained.

Once, he wrote that World War III was imminent. He said he'd been to Australia on vacation and discovered that the Russians were cornering the market on Australian sheep. They always did this before a big war, Seymour wrote, to line the coats of their soldiers. But the real tragedy was all those defenseless sheep being slaughtered.

Tom White called me into his office to show me Seymour's raw copy on the World War III scare. Then he killed the column. Then, having dispatched of the war fever, he marched into the sports office and handed over his first bet of the day.

And always, in the big, dank, cluttered newsroom, the phones were ringing, connecting everybody inside with people outside who seemed to dance along the fringes of noisy desperation.

"I'm calling to tell you I'm going to kill myself," a woman declared one Saturday night.

"Why?" I asked as gently as possible.

"I've been married for 36 years," she said, "and just discovered my husband is a homosectional."

Another woman called to announce, "There's a flying saucer over my house."

"How do you know it's a flying saucer?" I asked.

"Because," she replied in a voice that implied I was an idiot, "it's the same one that was over my sister's house last week."

The paper gave out $50 for the best news tip of the week. Readers bought police radios and monitored them, phoning in the latest hold-ups, fires, homicides. One time a guy called to say his brother-in-law was cutting the grass and had suffered a heart attack. The reporter taking the call didn't want to be rude about such a piffling news item, and said he'd need some more information.

"Not right now," the man on the other end shouted. "I've gotta call an ambulance."

Everybody in the newsroom stifled a laugh. But, behind the laughter was a lesson: People grabbed their shot when they could. Maybe it was money talking, and maybe it was a whole lifetime of feeling out of step, or feeling furious.

When Martin Luther King was assassinated and riots erupted, editors sent us into the streets for four days and nights. People were grabbing their shot: It was King's death, but it was also generations of rage finally finding an opening.

And, with the city on fire, there were other lessons. A curfew had been imposed, and I watched as the police grabbed teenagers by the hundreds and questioned them. Inevitably, every dialogue was the same:

Police: "Where are you going?"

Teenager: "My mother's."

Police: "Where are you coming from?"

Teenager: "My father's."

Something was going on out here that I hadn't heard about in my world, which had to do with families coming undone. The paper began giving me some flexibility—one day in the district courts, the next into the city jail, then into neighborhoods where I'd never been. A world was opening up.

I went to Fort Avenue in South Baltimore and discovered a neighborhood structured around certain basics: the corner bars, the American Legion post, the athletic fields where the kids played ball and the parents pulled out their lawn chairs to sit and chatter about life on the block.

In East Baltimore's Highlandtown, there was a front-stoop culture. Generations of men finished high school, or didn't quite, and marched off to the factories like Sparrows Point where they made steel or McCormick's where they made spices. They made a living comfortable enough to encourage their kids to follow them. Nobody talked about college. Such business was for upstarts, for downtown people, for the ones who'd never tossed a spitball in class when the teacher had her back turned.

I spent a year writing about the South Baltimore community of Cherry Hill. Heroin traffic was ruining what had been a middle-class black neighborhood, and in the places where white men held power, no one seemed particularly to notice.

"Drugs in Cherry Hill?" a city councilman said when my stories started running. "Cherry Hill? That's not even in the city, is it?" It is. He walked away, dismissing the stories and the problem.

"Drugs?" said a federal prosecutor. "Drugs are in the deepest ghetto. We can contain it there," effectively dismissing the coming cancer in poor black America.

A city, and a nation, was deluding itself. On Pennsylvania Avenue in West Baltimore, I asked a junkie one day, "How much dope do you put in your arm?"

"About $60 a day," he said. This was 1970.

"Where do you get the money?"

"I baby-sit for my cousin," he said, kissing me off.

An honest answer came from two junkies in Cherry Hill I got to know pretty well, little guys, strictly street hustlers. Stealing, they said. You steal something, and you sell it to somebody else. If it's something big, you take it to a fence and let him sell it for you.

"What do you mean, big?" I asked in my naïveté. "Like, an electric typewriter?"

"No," the first one said. "Like a Xerox machine."

The paper sent me into prisons that were filling beyond capacity with those whose drug habits sent them there. First time inside the state penitentiary, I met an inmate named Fred Hutchinson, whom everyone called Big Jake.

"How long you in for?" I asked, trying to make a little small-talk without specifically asking what he'd done. It seemed a kind of prison etiquette.

"I got life-plus-20," he said.

"Man," I said, "that's a long time."

"Yeah," said Big Jake, laughing out loud. "I still haven't figured out how I'm gonna serve that 20 yet."

Inside a lot of tragedies, there were ironic little laughs, and lessons to be tucked away. In South Baltimore, there was a guy named Eddie who seemed to hover around the edges of the drug traffic. He spotted me on the street one day and pulled over in a new Cadillac.

"Nice car," I said. "I guess I know where you got the money for it."

He looked genuinely hurt. "No," he said, "I've gone straight. I'm not into drugs any more."

"What are you into?" I asked.

"Numbers," he said.

Thus, another lesson: Always, a sense of perspective. There was crime that was shameful, and crime that came with a wink—just as there were politicians who talked honestly to you, and those who required simultaneous translation.

I started writing a column in January 1976, and three years and one month later moved it from the *News American* to the Baltimore *Sun*.

When I started the column, the governor of Maryland, Marvin Mandel, was about to be indicted, thus putting him in the company of several county executives, state legislators, and various other local politicians. It was easy to paint a broad picture of all politicians as thieves or fools.

At city hall, they simply seemed to have come from some other world. I'd grown up on the idealistic rhetoric and impossible good looks of the Kennedys. At Baltimore City Hall, there was Mayor William Donald Schaefer, who was asked one day for his political philosophy.

"I can sum it up in a single word," he declared, missing by only two. "People and caring."

In the city council, there was Clarence "Du" Burns, who'd spent years as a towel attendant in the Dunbar High School locker room; Dominic "Mimi" DiPietro, a second-grade dropout who ran into trouble each time he attempted to surround an idea with the English language ("The problem with the court system," he said one day, "is too much flea bargaining"); and Dominic Leone, who shot craps in his office during slack time.

Also, there was a former mayor, Tommy D'Alesandro, who was still around.

Every election day, Tommy the Elder was the first to cast his vote at School No. 2, in Little Italy. "Sacramental ground," he called it. Then in the evening, it was his job to count the neighborhood's votes. I grabbed him when Schaefer ran for re-election against attorney Billy Murphy.

"What was the count in Little Italy?" I asked.

"Schaefer, 487 to 1," said D'Alesandro.

"487 to 1?" I repeated incredulously.

"Yeah," said D'Alesandro very slowly, "and we're gonna find that guy."

But who were all these other guys, arriving from jobs in high school locker rooms, arriving with so little grip on the English language, arriving with dice in their hands?

I'll tell you who they were: Too unsophisticated to fake it. They weren't like those national politicians on television, the ones who'd learned to dress like corporate executives and talk like anchormen. They were the ones who'd grown up understanding they weren't the most brilliant kids in the class, or the handsomest, and so they'd learned to spot their openings. And when they'd gone to the voters sitting on the front steps and the bar stools and the little league fields in their neighborhoods, the voters looked at them and saw an image of themselves: Nobody very slick, nobody pretentious. They were ordinary people who hadn't learned how to hide their vulnerabilities, or didn't much care about them. They were people like themselves, who felt marginalized by the system and wanted a piece of it.

Schaefer might have been shaky on his arithmetic, but he took a beaten city and brought it back to life. Du Burns, the gentlest of men, helped reach across color lines in the edgy years after the riots. He wound up being the city's first black mayor, and paved the way for the next one, Kurt L. Schmoke, who arrived at city hall via an Ivy League education, a Rhodes scholarship, and a stint as state's attorney. Mimi DiPietro and Dominic Leone, unschooled men, went with their strengths: They were always on the telephone or in the neighborhoods, helping people who needed a job, getting the trash collected, fixing a playground at a school.

It was a city of working-class people, "the kind who built all the great cities, and nobody remembers it," said a city councilwoman named Barbara Mikulski one day long before she became a U.S. senator. She was in an angry mood, talking about a Yankee patrician America that had looked down its collective nose at working-class ethnics. "We were never accepted," she said. "They ridiculed our names, and our language, and our customs. The banks discriminated against us, and so did the colleges. We called ourselves Americans. They called us 'wop' and 'polack.' "

So the city comes with a defensive underlay, a suspiciousness of the white-bread types who came before and tried to keep them in their place. What evolves then is a determination to go your own way. You do this, as a community, by embracing in ever more fervent ways the things that are familiar. You do this, as an individual, by marching to your own beat. If the great sleek set doesn't want you, who needs 'em? You thumb your nose at those who don't understand the city's charms, and the thumbing becomes an act of mental health.

Though Baltimore spent much of the last half of the 20th century as a city with a mass inferiority complex, we started to get over it. We learned to accept our little idiosyncracies, and even flaunt them. Many who sprinkle their conversations with the East Bawlamer accent ("Upper Chesapeake adenoidal," to the sophisticates) do it with a good-natured sense of parody. Even radio disc jockeys, newly arrived from somewhere Out There, learn to speak the local patois well enough to announce, in warm weather, that folks are going "danny ayshin," which translates as "down the ocean." We've lived long enough to see ourselves glorified on movie screens by the hometown poet laureates Barry Levinson and John Waters. But it's a city wrestling with harsh modern problems: a population that contains most of the state's poor, its elderly, and its dangerous; a lot of kids from broken families who are running loose with guns and drugs; a public school system that, for all its best intentions, has graduated too many kids who are semiliterate. It's not entirely the schools' fault, either. They've got the kids for 6 hours a day, and the world has them for 18 hours.

And it's a city still wrestling with all the American edginess of race relations. Beginning in the mid-'50s, the great exodus to suburbia took thousands of white families out of the city, and later thousands of middle-class black families, leaving behind people who have only belatedly, and sometimes reluctantly, and not always successfully, learned to live with one another. It's an ongoing process.

A city is made up of communities. It's less a melting pot than a mosaic. When Schaefer was mayor, he took over a dispirited place, down in its heart and its pocketbook, depressed by the riots, and taught it to believe in itself. He always talked about neighborhoods. From them, he said, came a sense of belonging.

The syndicated columnist Garry Wills used to live here. One night he told a few friends the story of covering an antiwar protest in Washington, where he was swept up with a crowd of protesters and shoved toward police vans. Suddenly, out of nowhere, appeared John Waters and a camera crew, taking pictures for some later movie. The police thought they were a TV news crew.

"He's all right," Waters airily informed the cops, motioning toward Wills. "He's with us."

Wills has since moved out of town. But he told his listeners that night, "Ever since that day in Washington, I've always told myself, if I ever get in trouble, I keep thinking somebody from Baltimore will pop up and say, 'It's OK. He's with us.' "

You don't have to explain any of this to a Du Burns or a Barbara Mikulski, or to those in a back yard behind Streeper Street or a neighborhood bar on Fort Avenue.

You just look at your neighbor and say, "It's OK. He's with us."

CHARACTERS

The Gods of Mischief

In the waning years of the 20th century, it's become fashionable to call big cities unlivable. Those who remain in the places like Baltimore thus develop a variety of philosophical justifications: We love the neighborhoods, we love the mix of people, we love the energy. We keep repeating these things, like some urban mantra, and wonder if anyone ever believes us since, in our bleakest moments, we aren't always certain we believe ourselves.

This city can break your heart, but also lift it in the next instant if you stick around long enough to let it. The savvy Baltimoreans know about burglar alarms, car alarms, and the best streets to avoid. They also know there are actual neighborhoods where the outside world doesn't shut down just because the street lights come on and it's muggy outside. Twilight's just a signal to send the kids down to the corner for snowballs, which everybody will eat while they chat on the front stoops till about midnight. Or it's a signal that pickup basketball games will commence, now that the blazing sun's gone in, and that the games will go on all night long.

Does that make up for the crushing property taxes, the fear of gunplay, the schools where kids learn just enough math to measure a kilo? In tangible terms, absolutely not. And the truth is, you can live in scores of city neighborhoods and never go near a snowball stand or an all-night pickup basketball game, and it doesn't entirely matter.

What matters is that you know these things are out there, and it's nice, even at some physical distance, to feel that you belong to it, and you can partake in it if you get the urge. Living in this city, or in any American city at this time, is an act of faith. It's an embrace of crowded places, the clinging to notions of the melting pot, the close-up exchange of ideas, the energy that doesn't quit. We know it doesn't always work, and we sometimes feel like a vanishing tribe of believers, but we think that cities have to be made to work if America is to work.

It's been my great blessing to write about these things for a living. There are days that are marvelous fun, and days of despair, yet each is still a blessing. It's a front row seat at the world of the living.

Think of this first chapter as a sampler, a quick look at a variety of days and nights. In the life of all cities, change is the only constant. To cover it is, inevitably, to watch some of it making its earliest appearance and some of it taking a final bow.

A NORMAL DAY IN DISTRICT COURT

The big news out of Southeastern District Court yesterday morning: There is no big news. Just a kid caught getting high on paint fumes right there on the police station parking lot, a lady with a swastika on her arm allegedly soliciting a truck driver on Eastern Avenue, a woman who looks like a refugee from a Wagnerian opera who shot her boyfriend in a major area of his trousers, and the case of the hot-pants burrito. In the district courts of Baltimore City, this is known as an ordinary day. If news is the unusual, and reporters are connoisseurs of strangeness, then there is no news here.

"Why don't you come down here on a day when we've got something interesting?" Judge Robert J. Gerstung asks a visitor, at morning's end.

It's all in a day's work to Gerstung. In two hours, he'll handle 38 criminal cases, none of which will raise his eyebrows one iota. Here and there, a look of bemusement will crinkle his round, crew-cut features. He'll offer a homily to some offenders, delivered partly in earnest and partly with sarcastic overlay, as a kind of pressure-valve release for his own sense of the absurd. If a defendant ticks him off, he might take it a step further.

A while back, for instance, Gerstung gave a guy a year in prison. As guards led him out of the courtroom, the guy suddenly had an attack of attitude. "One year," he shouted. "Big deal. I can do that standing on my head."

Gerstung signaled to the guards to bring this bright lad back in front of the bench. "I'm gonna give you one more year," the judge declared drily, "to get you back on your feet."

But, big news? In the district courts? It's a system that handles nearly 80 thousand cases a year. That is no misprint. In order to avoid choking on its own backlog, judges are forced to toss out thousands of cases a year. In order to keep their sanity, they look for little pieces of human irony.

One day there was the high-fashion lady marched to the witness stand on charges of solicitation.

"Tell the court your name, please," said a city prosecutor named Brooke Murdock.

"Miss Nicole Longet," said the lady, speaking in a rapid-fire French accent.

"Has this always been your name?"

"No."

"What was your name before?"

"Leonard Young," explained Nicole Longet.

On this particular day in Southeastern district, the lady in question is also no particular lady. She's charged with shooting her boyfriend in the trousers. She's a large woman who looks as though she's been pulled off the bow of a clipper ship. The charge is assault with intent to murder. But the key witness, the boyfriend, is not in court. He's still in the hospital, reportedly resting comfortably.

How long will he be in the hospital? There's a certain amount of uneasiness over this one, a shifting of everyone's feet. Then, almost in a mumble, an attorney is explaining: "He was shot in the, ah, family jewels, judge."

Gerstung's eyes begin to roll heavenward, then stop. An idea has come into his head, a little self-defense mechanism to ward off the outrageousness. "Well," he says, "he can always sing in the choir." Moments later, a woman stands before him, charged with soliciting a truck driver on Eastern Avenue. She has a history of this kind of thing. She wears a sleeveless blouse over her chunky frame, and has a swastika tattooed on her arm.

A mistake has been made, she explains. The driver is merely a friend of hers. They were discussing world problems. The stock market, Gerstung suggests, or perhaps the possibility of a female appointment to the Reagan administration. Since the truck driver is a friend, he says, bring him to court and let him testify, and we'll see if we can work this out.

That's the essence of the district courts: Let's be practical. Forget the subtleties of the law books. That's for people with time on their hands. In the districts, the doors are always revolving too quickly, the streets keep coughing up all these wayward souls.

Take the defendant from the 7-Eleven on South Broadway. The guy running the 7-Eleven is a Korean fellow with a pretty heavy accent. The defendant is a Cuban fellow who speaks no English but has a friend attempting to do simultaneous translation. Out of this jumble of language, Gerstung must find justice.

It's a spicy case. The public defender, Bob Blatchley, calls it the Case of the Hot-Pants Burrito. Seems the defendant walked into the place at 1:30 in the morning, strolled to the rear, got a burrito out of the freezer, and then slipped it into the microwave oven.

A burrito is a Mexican delicacy that is shaped not unlike a thick hot dog. The defendant, looking to sneak it out of the store, takes the burrito out of the microwave and stuffs this steaming thing down the front of his pants.

The description takes everyone's breath away for a moment. Everyone is visualizing this scene. Nobody knows what to say.

Even Gerstung: "Only Mae West had a line for this," he says.

And they won't print it in a family newspaper.

AUGUST 5, 1984

NO LIFE LIKE CITY LIFE

On Streeper Street in Southeast Baltimore this glorious afternoon, the gods of mischief reach out to Theresa Koenig, and she welcomes them happily.

She has her family gathered in the back yard, husband John and the seven kids and various in-laws and cousins, plus neighbors from down the block. Somebody's gone over to Bud's for a bushel of crabs, and somebody else has walked over to Horsefeathers Pub for beer and sodas, and they've spread old newspapers for the crabs across a table in the little yard that runs next to the alley between Streeper Street and Kenwood Avenue.

All of this is quintessential Baltimore, except for one thing: Sitting in the yard is Theresa Koenig's 36-year-old nephew, Mike Pupek. He is from Pennsylvania. Theresa looks at her nephew, and as her family devours the last of their bushel of crabs, the gods of mischief whisper in her ear.

"Get him," they say in a kind of puckish chorus.

Theresa leaves the yard and goes into the kitchen, where she slices up a huge watermelon. Now she carries some of the watermelon into the yard. She has a gleam in her eyes. As she approaches her nephew Mike from behind, her husband John looks up and hollers, "Theresa, what are you doing?"

Already, he knows. From behind, Theresa reaches this huge piece of watermelon around her nephew Mike's head, until it's right in front of his face, and in one motion she commences one of the great watermelon smooshes of our time, a smoosh that keeps going until it covers his entire face, a kind of Baltimore hello to her out-of-town nephew.

Now all kinds of things begin to happen in the yard. Some scream loudly and take up battle stations. More watermelon is flung hither and yon, and then hither again. Now nephew Mike finds a back yard hose and hits Theresa in the face with water, and then he commences to spray at random. No prisoners will be taken. Neighbors on both sides of the alley see the Great Watermelon Battle in all its fury, and decide, "This looks like fun." They turn on their own hoses. They go to their own refrigerators and charge back outside carrying fruity weapons of war, and with comical whoops of abandon many of them fill balloons with water and begin heaving them back and forth across the alley.

This is the city of Baltimore having a little fun with itself.

On Streeper Street, the row houses are bunched tightly and have marble steps. Within one square block, you have not only Block's Pharmacy, JK's Grocery and Deli, Horsefeathers Pub, and John's Quality Bakery, but the lush Patterson Park, with its bicyclists, its ice rink, its swimming pool, its lovers strolling the lanes, its softball players of white collar and blue collar, of white skin and black skin, still nurturing athletic dreams long past the age of big league discovery.

"I always think of the laughter here," says Kathy Koenig, Theresa's daughter. She's 33, and she's moved away a few times, but she's back living in the neighborhood. Around here, that happens a lot. Kids grow up, and they make the big, emotional move out of their parents' home. Where do they move? Up the street.

Also, says Kathy Koenig, "Around here, you come out of the house after supper and you move from one neighbor's front steps to the next. It's not being nosy, it's just people looking for a little conversation."

And right there is the secret joy of city living: We all want a little company. In the dwindling days of the 20th century, everybody talks about the death of communities, which fell victim to television and air conditioning. Television isolates everybody with a piece of yapping furniture. Air conditioning took everybody off the street.

In the places like Southeast Baltimore, it's still a front-stoop culture, still a place where people's lives are intimately touched by their neighbors'. Is there crime in the city? Yeah, but down here we can talk about it. Are the Birds on a losing streak? Yeah, but c'mon over to the park and we'll hit a ball around for a while. Is the cost of living too high? Yeah, but . . .

But it's a community of small pleasures, of moving from one neighbor's front stoop to another, of hanging out for a beer at the corner bar, of finding out which kids have grown up and moved from one end of the block all the way to the other.

And, when the timing is right and the gods of mischief are having their way, of gathering the family in the back yard, and bestowing upon a nephew from out of town what's known in the trade as a Baltimore hello.

AUGUST 19, 1990

NORMA CLAYPOOL OPENS THE WORLD

In the beginning, there was Elaine.

The year was 1967, and Elaine was two years old and totally blind when Norma Claypool put her arms around the little girl and adopted her.

Then there was Kenny. He was born eight years ago, mentally retarded. Nobody wanted him. Norma did. She took him home when Kenny was seven months old.

Richard was next. He had one eye, which was capable of light perception, and what the doctors call a bilateral cleft face, an open furrow extending through his lip to his eye sockets. Richard was a year old when Norma embraced him.

Jothi was one of the homeless children of India—no disabilities, but no parents, either—when Norma found her through a Canadian adoption agency two years ago. Jothi's 13 now.

And then there's Noel. She's nearly four. She's been with Norma since midsummer. She's autistic. She lies in her bed, and she cries, and she shows almost no sign of wanting to walk or talk.

This is Norma Claypool's family. She is 51 and single. She is courageous and big-hearted beyond words, and there is one thing more. She is totally blind.

She laughs easily when you mention it. "People think I'm either wonderful or crazy," she says. "They say, 'I hope these children are grateful for you.' I say I'm grateful for the children."

Born in Pittsburgh, the youngest of six children, Norma was left sightless at two by a malignant tumor, known as retinoblastoma. She had no sight, only visions of what she wanted to do with her life.

She graduated high school but found her family had no money for college. So she worked as a stenographer for seven years, saved her money, and went to the University of Pittsburgh. She graduated magna cum laude. She did it in two and a half years.

"I had to do it fast," she says. "It was all the money I had."

Then she got her master's degree, and then her doctorate. And she would go on to teach special education courses for 10 years at Coppin State College. One former student recalls, "She was an excellent teacher, and she expected more than most teachers do. She wouldn't take any excuses. And you didn't come to class late, and try to sneak in. She could tell who you were just by the sound of your footsteps."

Norma sloughs off this kind of talk, saying she'd rather talk about her children than herself. "Now, Elaine," she says. "She's at Northern High. She's had all her education with seeing children. I don't want her competing with concessions. If she does, what happens when she goes to work? Nobody makes concessions for you there.

"Elaine discovered she was blind when she was almost four. She was sitting on my lap, and we had the TV on. We were listening to it. And there was a kitten on the show, and my mother said, 'What a cute kitten.' And Elaine said, 'Let me see it.' Of course, she meant, let me touch it. But when she touched the screen, there was just glass. And that's when it first hit her."

Kenny was born with Down's syndrome. At eight, he swims, rides a bike, plays with neighbors. But he has a bad heart. Richard's undergone four major operations on his face, and there are more to come. Norma says he's so bright he takes everyone's breath away. "We were talking about heaven one day, and he said, 'Momma, one day Jesus will reach down and pick Kenny up and take him to heaven. But not me. I'll have to be good.' In other words, he was telling me that Kenny's not accountable for what he does, but he is."

One day he asked Norma why he was born with one eye when everyone else came with two.

"I don't know," she told him.

"What's wrong with my face?" he asked.

"It's crooked. It just came out that way, honey, but it can be fixed."

"Will it hurt?"

"Yes."

"But I'll have a normal face?"

"Yes."

She doesn't believe in bending the truth with them, because no one else will. Late at night, she looks at Noel, autistic, asleep in her bed.

"I didn't take her on deliberately," she says. "I thought she was gonna be a nice retarded child. I like retarded children. But she's here now. It's like she's mine biologically. What am I gonna do, return her? She's my daughter."

All of this is said in matter-of-fact tones. She says it's a matter of life style. She says she likes children. None of them came with any government subsidies. She supported them completely on her teaching salary, until her voice gave out. Now there are disability payments and medical assistance.

But no assistance can match what Norma Claypool has given: simple human love for souls the rest of the world seemed to have forgotten.

NOVEMBER 8, 1981

BEEHIVE HAIRDOS AND BUDDY DEANE

If memory serves from a distance of about 25 years, I heard about the tragedy of the girl with the perfect beehive hairdo from my next-door neighbor Geri, who heard about it from her friend Fishsticks across the street, who heard about it from Rob who lived down on the corner, who heard it at school from a kid named Dink.

Beyond that, I can't trace it. Nobody in my neighborhood actually knew the girl with the beehive hairdo tragedy, but everybody in Baltimore seemed to know somebody who knew somebody who knew the story. If you grew up in the '50s, chances are you heard it, too, and probably even believed it, such were the times. It went like this:

This girl had managed to wrap her hair into a perfect beehive. Proud of it, she kept spraying it and spraying it, never bothering to wash it again. Of course not. What mattered personal hygiene if it meant losing the perfect hairdo?

Anyway, legend had it, bugs began living in her hair. After about six months, with the girl somehow not even realizing they were in there, the bugs naturally ate through to her brain and killed her.

Moral of the story, declared everyone's parents: Wash your hair or die.

Hey, it was the '50s, what did you expect? The '50s was a decade so uptight and boring it actually lasted 13 years, until the Kennedy assassination in 1963. John Waters was around then. Now he's made a movie about the era, called *Hairspray,* his slightly demented look at 1962, when the '50s were beginning to be over.

Naturally, being of that time, he remembered the girl with the beehive hairdo when making his movie. He didn't actually know her, of course, but he knew somebody who knew somebody . . .

"Of course, of course," he was saying yesterday morning, hours before his movie's premiere. "Everybody heard that rumor. That's why, in the movie, they keep talking about roaches in her hair. Back then, everybody had that kind of hairdo."

Especially, everybody on the *Buddy Deane Show,* the local version of Dick Clark's *American Bandstand* dance show, which is brought vividly back to life in the movie.

"There was a girl named Kathy on the show who had a great beehive that resembled a trash can sitting on top of her head," Waters remembered, "and Pixie, who was barely five feet tall but her hair added a good six to eight inches to her height. You could throw her hair down to the ground, and her hair would crack."

Waters has always called Baltimore the hairdo capital of the world, though he was chagrined recently to see a newspaper story claiming Salt Lake City uses more hairspray per capita than any place in the country.

"What can I tell you?" he said. "Mormons like 'dos. But Baltimore still has to have more beauty parlors per capita than anywhere in the world. Go to East Baltimore, go to Dundalk, Highlandtown, Middle River. Chris Mason, who did the hair for the movie, said something about when you find a good look, you stick with it for the rest of your life."

Naturally, this brings Waters back to Buddy Deane, the foundation for a TV show in *Hairspray.* The show was a daily barometer of hair hipness, all those guys with hair slicked back like jet streams, all those girls with the beehives and the bouffants, the looks weaving themselves so firmly into the culture that there are still parts of East and South Baltimore where they've never gone away.

"Yetta and Gretta Kotik," Waters remembers. They were Buddy Deane Committee members with great, teased hair. "And Mary Lou Raines, the Annette Funicello of the show," who seemed to have a different hairstyle for every day of the decade: the Double Bubble, the Artichoke, the Airlift, the hair first getting sprayed, then getting toilet papered and blotted.

"Mary Lou," Waters says now, with great comic reverence, "was hair-hopper royalty."

From royalty, Waters knows. Working with limited budgets, he's never been able to cast the biggest names in Hollywood, but sometimes he gets yesterday's stars. It gives them a paycheck, and it gives Waters's movies a campy, in-joke kind of look.

Once, he tried to get Blaze Starr for one of his films. Blaze, legendary when she stripped at the Two O'Clock Club on The Block, still lives in the area. Her sister acts as her agent. Waters called.

"Is there any nudity involved?" the sister asked.

"No," Waters assured her, thinking to himself that Blaze must be pushing 60.

"Well, then," said the sister, "she wouldn't be interested then."

"Strippers," Waters was saying now, getting ready for tonight's big premiere. "They still have to show it, even if no one wants to look."

But Blaze wouldn't have fit *Hairspray*. Waters calls it "a satire of the two most dreaded film genres today, the teen flick and the message movie. It could be my breakthrough. I'm saying prayers to the hairdo gods."

FEBRUARY 23, 1988

MIMI TURNS 80

One day Mimi DiPietro and I go for a ride in his brand new shiny automobile.

"What did you buy a Cadillac for?" I ask.

"Are you kidding?" he says. "This thing will last me 10 years."

"Yeah, but what happens after that?" I ask.

"After that, we'll see," says Mimi.

He was 75 years old at the time. It's nice for 75-year-old people to have 10-year plans. The conversation took place five years ago. A few months ago, Mimi decided the car was getting too old and traded it in, which is another way of saying he outlived it.

He bought another shiny new Cadillac. He figures it ought to last him another 10 years. After that, we'll see.

On Friday, Dominic "Mimi" DiPietro, rotund First District Baltimore City councilman, the only man who ever simultaneously greeted President Jimmy Carter and Pope John Paul by grabbing the back of the president's pants and referring to the pontiff as "Mister Pope," the man who causes listeners to swoon when he surrounds an idea with the English language, turned 80.

They had a birthday party for Mimi at Tiffany's, the East Baltimore hall owned by his friend Buddy Paolino. Rep. Barbara Mikulski was there, and declared, "In 1904, Baltimore had a fire. In 1905, God gave us Mimi to rebuild the city." Rep. Helen Bentley brought a birthday card from Ronald and Nancy Reagan, addressed to the unofficial "Mayor of Highlandtown." And Mayor William Donald Schaefer, who was there the day it happened, talked of that wonderful moment on the White House lawn when Mimi, in his irrepressible way, gave a Baltimore hello to the president of the United States and the pope.

But before we get to that, a few words from our sponsor . . .

Mimi DiPietro, on his personal popularity: "More people know me now than ever and I have been to a half a dozen political affairs lately and each time I get a standing evasion."

Mimi on an old friend: "I knowed him from the time he used to sing in the church quarry."

Mimi on lying: "I would never tell a lie. If I have to lie to you, I'll deviate from you."

Mimi doing a political tour of The Block and gazing into a peep show booth, and then gently dropping a quarter in a film slot to observe (strictly, of course, from a political perspective): "Now I'd like to have that done to me, and who don't is not a damned human

being. But I understand that young men are going in here and degener-
ating."

But leave us return now to Tiffany's on Friday night, and thence to
the Jimmy Carter White House and the pope.

Here was Mayor Schaefer, still shaking his head in woozy disbelief
after all this time, declaring: "It was an amazing experience to everybody who witnessed it. To grab the president, and not get shot by the
Secret Service. And then, to have the president introduce him to the
pope, and Mimi's talking about alleys in East Baltimore."

Imagine the scene: Campaigning for the presidency, Carter had
come here and met DiPietro, who mentioned that the streets and alleys
of East Baltimore were not what they should be, and if Carter wanted
his support, why, he'd have to have a serious street and alley plank in
the platform.

Carter gets elected, and now it's three years later, and when Pope
John Paul II comes to the White House, Carter invites a lot of promi-
nent Catholics in and out of government, including Mimi DiPietro of
Baltimore.

Everyone wants to get near the president, and everyone wants to get
near the pope. Mimi has mixed feelings. There is a woman who wants
to see the pope, a handicapped woman who would like his blessing.
Mimi decides to look out for her.

On the White House lawn, all the people are crying, "Poppa, poppa,
over here, poppa," while Secret Service agents swarm everywhere as the
president and the pontiff weave back and forth through the crowd.

And here comes Mimi, in a gleaming yellow suit, and he sneaks up
behind the president and grabs him by the waistband and pulls upward,
the old policeman's trick for giving the bum's rush, where if you start
struggling, you wind up a candidate for the Vienna Boys Choir.

"Hey, Mister President, you remember me?" says Mimi, hand on the
president.

"Mimi DiPietro of Baltimore," says Jimmy Carter, remembering immediately, and then turns to introduce him to the pontiff.

But Mimi, remembering the handicapped lady, says:

"Mister Pope, take care of this lady. She needs you, I don't."

And then, blithely turning back to Carter, he says, "Three years ago
you come to Baltimore when you wanted to be president. You promised

me money to fix up my streets and alleys and I'm still waitin', Mister President, I'm still waitin'."

Naturally, at his birthday party Friday, Mimi modestly downplayed the incident. He said, "I had him by his belt is all. And there was FBI guys around. All I did was two times I shoved him. And somehow or other, I don't know, God made the president of the United States bring the pope to me."

The last time Mimi talked to Jimmy Carter, it was different. Carter asked him how his health was. And Mimi called him a name. "I called him an SOB," he admitted. " 'Cause, what the hell, I don't need him, he lost."

Mimi DiPietro: He outlives Cadillacs. And presidents, too.

MARCH 24, 1985

BOOGIE RETURNS TO THE DINER

Everybody can't wait to see Leonard "Boogie" Weinglass on a movie screen. Larger than life, Boogie's always been. Narrow enough to fit into a movie story, never.

But there he is, in the new Barry Levinson movie, called *Diner*. It's about the old Hilltop Diner, on Reisterstown Road just below Rogers Avenue, and about five guys caught in the final moment between adolescence and adulthood, without particularly wanting to embrace either.

Among them is one called Boogie, played by the actor Mickey Rourke, whose character is described thusly: "The calm and smooth ladies' man ... the crowd's flashiest dresser ... by day he works in a beauty salon, but plans to move on to bigger things. In pursuit of these bigger things, he's made a 'sure' bet for $2,000 on the Colts-Giants championship game, even though he only has $50 to his name."

Clearly, this was a very long time ago. Nobody knows quite what the current Boogie is worth. But he's co-owner of the clothing chain called Merry-Go-Round, and his net worth is estimated to be approaching nine figures.

But, back in the winter of '59, when *Diner* takes place?

Oy.

Take the Night of the Missing Police Car, for example, which tells us nothing about his state of wealth but much about his state of mind.

Boogie was maybe 17 at the time but didn't have a driver's license. He and another guy were downstairs at Mandel-Ballow's old deli, right across the street from the diner, fighting and breaking up the furniture. The manager called the cops. Several squad cars pulled up as the fight was ending.

Boogie had beaten the other guy, and now he got up, straightened his clothing, and began walking calmly up the steps as the cops charged downstairs.

He strode right past the cops. He marched out to the parking lot, where he saw a wonderful thing: One of the police cars had its motor running. Boogie got into the car. He drove it away.

"It jumped and stuttered the whole way," Boogie was remembering yesterday. "I mean, I didn't drive a stick shift too well. I didn't even have a car till I was 30. I drove the car up Reisterstown Road, past Ameche's Drive-In. I was sick, because nobody was there. Man, I wanted to be seen.

"I had it out about an hour, and then I drove it back. The police picked me up the next morning. They knew it was me. They just knew."

At City College, where he matriculated between sessions at Knocko's poolroom, Boogie was admired for several reasons:

a. He was one of the best basketball players in the state.
b. He was the guy who had football pools for sale.
c. He was the guy who somehow had blank report cards for sale.

The story behind the blank report cards is simple enough. Boogie was constantly getting sent to Principal Henry T. Yost's office. Yost became so accustomed to seeing him there that he took his presence for granted. Once, Yost strolled into the hall. Boogie glanced down, saw a desk drawer sticking out, with this stack of report cards.

"It was a no-brainer," he explained yesterday. "I only made one mistake."

"What's that?" he was asked.

"I took all of them."

Those who didn't approach him for report cards knew they could reach him for football pools, those cards carrying the various point spreads for betting. There was the time, with City's varsity basketball team on the floor, in uniform, doing pregame warmups as the crowd cheered them on, when Boogie was outside the building, also in uniform, booking a few last-minute football bets.

Behind him came George Young, City's massive football coach who is now the New York Giants general manager. Young grabbed Boogie by the scruff of his neck. "What do you think you're doing?" Young demanded.

"Just trying to make a living," Boogie explained.

He married right out of high school, tried a fling at hairdressing, divorced at 22. Moved to Georgia, worked as a traveling salesman, then opened a head shop in Atlanta.

One head shop became four clothing stores. He came back to Baltimore, hooked up with Harold Goldsmith, and the stores took on a name: Merry-Go-Round. Now there are more than two hundred stores, and Boogie has four homes in three states, with neighbors who are movie stars and professional athletes.

"I'm leading the kind of life everybody wants to lead," he says. "When I started making money, I'd go out to the Woodholme Country Club here, and all these people had money, but nobody was having any fun. They didn't know how to enjoy life.

"I never had any money. My family was supported by charity. We lived on Violet Avenue, and my dad got TB when I was two years old and my mother was an immigrant. I had to hustle. I was known for my basketball, my dancing, and fighting. If you knew Boogie, you either liked him, or hated him, or you were scared of him."

And you knew he was larger than life, which is precisely how he's arrived, up there on a movie screen.

MARCH 10, 1982

A CHILD SHALL LEAD THEM

The first thing you notice are the little boy's hands, which are hugging the top of a brown paper bag of cookies. The little boy is no more than six. He's sitting next to his mother on the No. 8 bus that stops by the downtown campus of the University of Maryland as it travels east on Baltimore Street, and something is terribly wrong.

The boy sits in the aisle seat, and his mother is by the window, sleeping deeply. In the blue smoky glow of early evening, downtown traffic is clotted. On the No. 8 bus, people head home from work with eyes dull as stone. The boy with the bag of cookies looks wide eyed at the crush of people and the cars in the street, but he's also a little bit distracted.

He's leaning back against his mother. He puts all of his weight against her to keep her from falling over each time the bus turns. The mother is out-cold drunk, reeking of alcohol, snoring in tones ragged as a broken bottle.

It is clear that the mother has become the responsibility of the child.

The boy's hands work fiercely around the top of this brown paper bag now, holding it tightly, twisting it, reducing it to a thing in his life that he can control.

The mother is out of control. She's probably in her late 30s, but looks older. She is chubby, dressed in clothes that look as though they've been slept in. But at least she's upright—until the bus turns near the Old Town firehouse and the woman starts to fall over sideways.

The boy's hands twist fiercely at the top of the brown paper bag. He puts his feet in the aisle and props his whole body against his mother to hold her up. He looks undernourished, and his clothes hang from him like a collection of rumpled sacks, and he's losing his fight.

People look away in blushing discomfort. Standing in the aisle now, looking down at the boy, is a woman in her 40s. She has an armful of groceries and wears clothes that look like freshly ironed leftovers from an attic.

"Baby, is that your momma?" she asks the boy.

His eyes widen. He doesn't know this woman. He says yes, but his expression says, why are you asking?

"Do you know where your stop is?"

He shakes his head no.

"Do you know your address?"

"No."

"Well, try to wake your momma up," she says. Her voice is beyond quiet. It is tender, it caresses like velvet.

Now the boy leans into his mother and says, "Momma, Momma, wake up," gently pushing her. She doesn't budge. The boy looks up at the woman in the aisle, and she nods at him. He shakes his mother again, this time harder.

"Momma," he says. But she flops back and forth, like a puppet whose strings have been cut, and the boy braces her so she won't do it again, and leans on her and looks at the crowd on the bus looking back at him.

The bus has reached Greenmount Avenue now. The boy reaches into his brown bag, gets out large pieces of cookies, then twists the bag tight again. He chews on the cookies for a few moments, the hands again straining at the top of the bag, and then he turns back to his mother.

"Momma, wake up," he says. He shakes her, hits her hard on the shoulder with his bag, reducing the cookies inside to crumbs. He isn't angry, just increasingly anxious, and so hits her repeatedly.

In the gathering gloom, the bus stops every few blocks, and people get on who do not look at the little boy. Wrapped inside their own lives, their days have been difficult enough.

But now a girl, maybe 20, gets on the bus and seems to know the boy. "Wake your mother," she tells him.

The older woman in the aisle looks at her and asks, "Do you know them?"

"Yeah."

"Do you know where they live?"

"Yeah. Their street's coming up in a few blocks."

The older woman leans down now to nudge the boy's mother. The boy has given up. Out of energy, he leans on his mother and looks out the window, as though searching for escape routes.

Now the older woman in the aisle is getting edgy. She pushes the boy's mother hard, and slowly, painfully, in clumsy installments, she rouses her.

The mother is completely incoherent.

"You have to wake up," the older woman says. "You're home, and you have to take your baby home."

The bus is just above North Avenue now, heading up Greenmount. A third woman in the aisle, who has been watching, leans over, and now the three women help heave the boy's mother to her feet, and they get her off of the bus, stumbling down the back steps of the vehicle.

Nobody on the bus looks back. As it pulls away, the woman stands on Greenmount Avenue, teetering badly, totally unaware of where she is.

And the little boy is standing next to her, wondering what he will do now.

DECEMBER 12, 1979

"HON" IS WHERE THE HEART IS AT

Somewhere out there—Patapsico Abnew in Souf Bawlamer? Dancin' the polka onna payment in Dundock?—is a poet with a paintbrush and a sense of humor and the soul of the city pulsing through his or her veins.

You want evidence? Check the Bill Hotz photograph that ran on this newspaper's Maryland section front page two mornings ago. It's all about the national language of Baltimore, and the municipal psyche of the city.

It's a little sign in the median strip of the Baltimore-Washington Parkway, as you enter the city, which used to say:

WELCOME TO BALTIMORE

But now says:

WELCOME TO BALTIMORE, HON!

I think I just fell in love.

"Hon" is the verbal emotional center of Baltimore. Even in a time of great social transition and political upheaval—where many of us are first learning to eat quiche, even though we're still mispronouncing it— "hon" is still the common denominator of the mother tongue, a word that embraces all of us into the same community without asking first for name, rank, and zip code.

It's a counter lady at the Lexnin Market asking if you need a spyewn for your oystyer soup.

It's an unselfconscious intimacy that wouldn't understand officiousness if it got imported from Naplis or Warshnin.

It's legions of Bawlamoreans pressing down on our car exhilarators with pride as we had toward Norf Abnew or Hollantayon or even the Pratt Liberry.

And if the city of Baltimore doesn't leap into action and paint WEL-

COME TO BALTIMORE, HON on every available road sign, then everybody at city hall is paying even less attention than we imagine.

(Is this legitimizing graffiti? Of course. But understand something: Graffiti isn't just a visual intrusion. It's a reflection of the soul of the intruder. And this is a soul as reflective of Baltimore as crabs and beer or never getting over the loss of the Colts.)

WELCOME TO BALTIMORE, HON is the essence of this city. It's all about friendly unpretentiousness and not taking ourselves too seriously, and it's about a sense of home.

Robert Frost almost had it right, when he wrote: "Home is the place where / When you have to go there / They have to take you in."

Actually, if he'd been a Baltimorean, he'd have written, "Home is the place where / When you have to go there / They have to take you in at."

(This doesn't mean we don't know good grammar around here. Everybody in Baltimore knows, for instance, you got your singular *you* and your plural *youse*.)

But I digress. What Frost should have written was: "Home is the place where / When you have to go there / They ought to call you 'Hon.' "

WELCOME TO BALTIMORE, HON talks to everybody who has a heart that beats. It's an automatic smile, a roadside hug for hometowner and tourist alike.

This is a city uneasy putting on airs. Having shrugged off much of its historic municipal inferiority complex, it's still a little uncomfortable getting dressed up for company.

WELCOME TO BALTIMORE, HON says: "We don't think of you as company. We think of you as one of us, for as long as you feel like staying with us."

"Baltimoreans are likely to take the time not only to greet but to chat at some length with strangers who pop up in their lives," Tony Hiss writes in the current *New Yorker*. It's a long and affectionate piece on the town, which captures some of its essence but will make natives feel a little self-conscious knowing people around the country will be reading it.

What, somebody from New York's paying attention to us? Hon, you got nothin' better to do with your time than that?

"The air in Baltimore feels soft and gentle on your skin; the summers are tropical. In June, on open ground, there's a sharp, rich, enveloping smell, made up of honeysuckle and a dozen other flowering vines and shrubs."

That's Tony Hiss again, sounding like a poet. It's all very flattering, but we're a little self-conscious with poetry, which is too studied.

"Hon" is more our style, because it has no style. It's not studied, it just slips off the tongue. Is anybody at city hall listening? If they are, do they understand they've just been handed a public relations gift from the gods?

Welcome to your new city slogan, hons. It's as Bawlamer as you could get.

APRIL 25, 1991

ANGELOS'S HEART STILL BELONGS TO HIGHLANDTOWN

Peter Angelos is reclining like a fighter between rounds in his luxury suite at Camden Yards, with a waitress named Michelle hovering nearby, a luscious dinner menu awaiting his choosing, and various men in expensive suits hoping to grab little increments of his time when third baseman Chris Sabo sprawls to intercept a sharp ground ball on its way to left field.

"Chris Sabo," declares Angelos, waggling one finger in the air and issuing perhaps the ultimate compliment in his repertoire, "is Highlandtown."

He should know. The new Orioles owner is worth uncounted millions of dollars, and he's spending it left and right, but his heart never entirely left the blue-collar East Baltimore neighborhood where he grew up, where his personality was forged and where he still finds a frame of reference for the unpretentious, tough-minded qualities he treasures.

In other words, his current state being about as good as life gets, what with the Orioles generally winning and his family healthy and his law practice in high gear, he hasn't forgotten where it all began.

"I was a Highlandtowner," he was saying the other night, as the Orioles were edging the California Angels. "That tells it all. We took up for our rights. We might have provoked a few unfortunate fights, but we didn't pick on anybody. You know, you wouldn't fight to put a guy out of commission, it was just to get the job done. You'd hit hard, you'd make your point. And it was always strictly with fists. It'd be good to return to those days."

In ways that are important, he never exactly left. His style is still direct, no frills attached. It's his $173 million investment out there on the playing field, and he's charmed by it, but you sense there's a piece of Angelos chafing to get back to his law office, where there's serious action. He's a long way from Highlandtown, and yet he's not.

A few weeks ago, he met with Jack Kent Cooke, the wealthy and cantankerous owner of the Washington Redskins, who wishes to move his football team to Laurel, over Baltimore's dead body. The meeting took place in the congressional office of Helen Bentley. Better, they should have staged it in a back alley.

Angelos called Cooke a carpetbagger for trying to come into Maryland. Cooke threatened to buy a baseball team to compete with Angelos's Orioles.

"Good," said Angelos, "I like competition."

"So do I," said Cooke.

"The hell you do," said Angelos. "That's what this move to Laurel's all about. You want a monopoly."

The two men were drinking wine out of plastic cups, but not for long. Cooke got so upset, he snapped his cup and spilled wine on his expensive suit. Then he tried to intimidate Angelos, telling him he'd been checking him out. "I know more about you than you think," Cooke said.

"Then you must be very impressed," Angelos replied.

He should be. Angelos has always had different worlds tugging at him. There was the immigrant world of his parents versus the streets of East Baltimore. And then there was the choice of life after Patterson High School. Most of his old buddies headed for Sparrows Point's steel mills. Angelos went to the old Eastern College of Commerce and Law. "With my parents," he says, "college was a given. You had to go to college, and then go as far as money and nerve and energy would take you. My father only went to the third grade. His father was killed in a construction accident, and so my father had to go to work. My parents wanted more for me."

He always figured his working-class roots were a plus. Those who came out of Harvard Law School didn't understand the streets, hadn't come out of the same ethnic melting pot. When he emerged from night school, he threw himself into workmen's compensation cases, criminal defense, plus representation for Local 2610 of the Steelworkers Union.

In 1974, they started seeing hundreds of guys from Bethlehem Steel with the same problem: They'd been exposed to asbestos, and they were dying. The union's leadership asked him to represent about four hundred of these men. During the next 20 years, four hundred became ten thousand cases, people from steel mills, from shipyards, what Angelos calls an immense tragedy.

"The manufacturers knew," he says softly. "For 40 years they knew this stuff was killing people, and they concealed it, and hundreds of thousands of people didn't know the deadly hazard they were facing." His voice grows softer now, so it isn't much louder than a whisper. "I've seen some terrible suffering," he says. "Too many people. A national calamity."

He has 65 attorneys and 135 backup people working on various cases. It makes his operation the largest plaintiffs' office in the country. And it's made Angelos wealthy beyond imagining.

When he bought the Orioles at auction, he remembers, "I didn't care how high the bidding went. In my mind, I knew I would go higher. I mean, I was thinking, 'When is this SOB gonna give it up?' But until he did, I wasn't leaving."

After Edward Bennett Williams's threats, after Eli Jacobs's icy distance, Angelos is, among other things, a huge relief to Baltimoreans: How nice, finally, to have somebody own the club who understands the town.

Here's an example: This is Tuesday night, the night Wild Bill Hagy makes his unexpected return to public life. In Angelos's suite, the first response is puzzlement. What's that roar sweeping the right field seats? Suddenly, people around Angelos are yelling, 'Wild Bill. It's Wild Bill.'"

No last names are necessary. Angelos's face lights with sheer joy. He knows the truth: His ballpark is filled every night, but it lacks the electricity of Memorial Stadium. Wild Bill and his beer have been muted by a crowd that includes too many D.C. yuppies bearing wine spritzers and *Wall Street Journals*. There's not enough buzz in the place.

"I've gotta talk to him," Angelos says. "I will talk to him. Wild Bill, how do you like that? He's got the whole place buzzing."

There's a sense that Eli Jacobs might have found Wild Bill an interloper, a blight on his fancy new digs. Angelos knows better. He understands not only baseball, but Baltimore. He's happy to have all the D.C. yuppies loving his ball club, but his heart belongs to a state of mind called Highlandtown.

APRIL 24, 1994

STREETS

**"Who Are These Super-rich People?
I Mean, What Are Their Names, and
What Are We Gonna Have to Do
When We Find Them?"**

You never know who you'll meet on the streets.

One day I'm on Washington Boulevard, and there's Wild Man Joe O'Connell, looking like it's the 1940s and he could climb back into a boxing ring tomorrow. Long ago, he fought professionally, if you use the term loosely. One time he boxed 10 rounds for $20. Another time, he fought out at Fort Howard and was paid with a carton of cigarettes. And Joe didn't even smoke. Once, he fought a gorilla for $50. He lost, but it was quick. Another time, he fought a kangaroo for a dollar a minute on a Pigtown parking lot. He made $8 before the kangaroo got serious.

Another day I'm on High Street, and there's Willie the Rug. The nickname comes from his toupee, which cost him $245 and looks like something pulled from a clogged drain. Everybody says Willie should ditch the rug. But he knows better. One night in a crap game at President and Fawn, the game gets raided and everybody loses their money to the cops, except for Willie. He hides his winnings. He hides them by slipping them under the rug, patting everything into place, and then informing the cops that he lost everything before they arrived.

One time on Eutaw Street there's a lady named Nancy, whose body seems to ripen in the noonday sun. She's with a fellow named Izzy, who wants to do something nice for his girlfriend.

"I need a coat this size," he says, running his hands down Nancy's contours.

"Any kind?" says Nancy.

"Something nice," says Izzy. "Go steal me something with class."

And then Nancy disappears across Eutaw, toward Howard Street where there are stores. And in no more than five minutes, no more time than it takes for Izzy to describe Nancy's drug habit that sends her daily into department stores to support her addiction, she reappears on Eutaw Street with a freshly stolen coat which, now that you mention it, does have a certain class.

Walk through East Baltimore, and it's pick 'em whether you find more pictures of Elvis or Jesus in people's living rooms. Walk through West Baltimore, and there are people who still worship at the shrine of Fat Daddy. He was a radio disc jockey, or maybe a god. In either case, he made thousands of white kids wish they'd been born black.

Every neighborhood has its own stories to tell, its own personality. Some of the streets have gotten mean. The city's got too many homeless, too many junkies, too many kids carrying guns. But each place carries its charms, too.

SIGN OF THE TIMES POINTS TO WIDENING GAPS

Look at this: Across the street from the Hollins Street Market in Southwest Baltimore, there are signs in adjoining windows.

One, in the Hollins Liquor Store, printed in bold lettering, says: "Play The Lottery."

The other, hand-lettered in the office window a few feet away next door, says: "Food Stamp Center Here. Come In. We're Open."

This is America in the dying years of the 20th century: people getting in one line to keep their heads above water, and then in another to dream of hitting it big once and living off the residuals for the rest of their lives.

"Oh, you should see it," says Joe Kuhn, who's 46 and laid off work and has lived here all his life. "Poor people get in line every day to play that number. You always know which ones are poor. They're the ones who bet the most money. They're looking for that one big hit to get out of poverty."

The odds say they're not going to make it. You want numbers? A report out of Washington, based on figures from the Congressional Budget Office, says in the bluntest language that we're increasingly becoming a nation of haves and have-nots.

In the 1980s, the gap between rich and poor widened so much that the wealthiest 1 percent of Americans now have virtually the same amount of money as the bottom 40 percent of the country. Ten years ago, the top 1 percent "only" made about half as much as the bottom 40 percent.

And, while this was going on, the share of income going to those in the middle class dropped to lower levels than any time since World War II.

Does any of this seem fair in a nation that theoretically prides itself on inclusion in the economic mainstream? Three cheers for capitalism and all that, but when does greed become a kind of knee-jerk obscenity, and when do multimillionaires say: I think I have enough. And when do poor people decide they've had enough, too?

In Southwest Baltimore yesterday morning, here was Bili Savage, president of the Hollins Market Neighborhood Association, and she was saying this: "I saw that report in the newspaper, and I was wondering, who are these super-rich people? I mean, what are their names, and what are we gonna have to do when we find them?"

Savage is 31 years old and works at the Cultured Pearl restaurant. She says she makes about $20,000 a year now. This means she lives from one paycheck to the next. It also means, in this neighborhood, that she is perceived as one who has made it big.

"What happens," she was saying now, "is a sense of anger and hopelessness. Most of the crime around here is breaking and entering and mugging. Classic drug crimes. You get kids breaking bottles on the street. All of this is frustration talking. There was a little girl outside church the other day, and she picked up a syringe she saw lying in the street. She's 3 or 4 years old, what does she know? The junkies are all over the place. Now she's gotta keep going to the hospital for AIDS tests."

In the 1000 block of West Baltimore Street now, here came a kid named Tony, riding his bicycle past a pay telephone that held three empty beer cans glistening in the morning sun.

"This is where I seen the man," says Tony. He is 10 years old. The man he saw was lying in the street with a bullet in his chest and his blood all over the sidewalk. "He tried to rob the potato chip man," Tony explains, "and the potato chip man had a gun in his truck and shot him. I saw him lying in the street."

"You see anything else?" Tony is asked.

"Needles," he says softly. "I see them all the time. My mom be saying not to touch them."

This puts Tony one step ahead of the little girl outside church, but many steps behind the rich of this country, about whom the report out of Washington says:

- The poorest 20 percent of the country lost 5 percent of their after-tax income during the last decade.
- The middle 20 percent gained about 3 percent— about $600.
- The top 1 percent gained about $186,000.

"I wish I could say this surprises me, but it doesn't," Katie O'Meara was saying yesterday. She was sitting at Rudy's Patisserie, across from the Hollins Street Market. "That's why they put all the lottery signs in this neighborhood. They make people think they've got a way out, when they don't. They'll put their money into the lottery and run out of money for living expenses. A lot of people around here don't even have phones in their house. Look at all the phones on the street. That's because the phones are the first thing to go when money gets tight."

Well, not quite the first. A sense of realistic hope goes before the phones do. A sense of being included in the American mainstream goes, and a sense of bitterness comes in, and then a subculture of anger grows and takes on a life of its own.

The new numbers out of Washington just put this into perspective. In Southwest Baltimore, among people with white skin as well as black, the numbers translate to food stamp and lottery lines side by side, and potato chip delivery men packing guns, and a three-year-old finding a syringe outside a church, left there by somebody who gave up long ago.

JULY 26, 1990

A CABBIE HAS HIS DAY

When last seen, Alan Blumenthal was on his way to jail on charges of going to the toilet. Yesterday, he returned to the scene of the crime. This time, it felt like a triumph.

The people who run the downtown Hilton Hotel had Blumenthal arrested last summer for going to the bathroom against their will. It's a public bathroom he used, but not intended for certain elements of the public. Cab drivers, for example. This is Blumenthal's problem. Next time he wants to use the facilities, he should first arrange for a different way to make a living.

But there he was, around 9:30 one morning last July, with a queasy stomach from some hamburgers he'd had the night before. He'd dropped a fare on Key Highway and returned to the hotel for another customer, when he realized he'd need the men's room.

In the eyes of the Hilton people, this created a problem: They don't like cab drivers entering their lobby.

"I understand the reasoning," Blumenthal says. "They don't want us coming in and soliciting customers. It'd be too raucous for a hotel."

Unfortunately, to get to the men's room in the Hilton, you have to go through the hotel lobby.

"I was very discreet," says Blumenthal. "The manager knows me, the bellman knows me. A lot of them know me, from getting passengers there. So I told them I had to use the toilet. They said I couldn't. I said, 'Look, I have diarrhea.' A special policeman followed me through the lobby and kept warning me, "Don't you use the toilet. Don't you use the toilet.' He actually followed me. And I went in, and closed the door, and sat down. And he said, 'Hurry up, you're under arrest.' "

When Blumenthal emerged, there were two security guards and a hotel manager there, and they pronounced him under arrest, hemming him in while Blumenthal went into what he calls his passive resistance stance until city police arrived, 20 minutes later.

The police, showing marvelous sensitivity and tact, put Blumenthal's hands behind his back, handcuffed him, and marched him through the hotel lobby to a police wagon while Blumenthal hollered to people, "This is what happens when you go to the bathroom at the Hilton."

And then he spent 11 hours in jail.

"The police will tell you I went a little crazy," Blumenthal says. "And I did. It was humiliating. They stripped me of all my clothes, which is how I sat there in my cell."

Yesterday, he got his revenge—sort of.

Five months after the fact, Blumenthal was there for his day in court, but nobody showed up from the Hilton. Thus, charges were dropped.

"An outrage," he called it. "I gave up a day's pay to be here. You know, when they arrested me, they offered me probation before verdict. But I said no. I said it meant I'd have to hold my bladder for a year, and I want to press this case."

So yesterday, he did the next best thing.

He walked out of the courthouse and up Calvert to Fayette, and then to the Hilton Hotel. There, he got a rousing welcome from cabbies parked outside the lobby. Then Blumenthal marched himself into the lobby, and took an elevator to the fourth floor, where General Manager Roland Schmidt was sitting in his office.

"What if I have to go to the bathroom?" said Blumenthal.

"Then go," said Schmidt. "We've changed our policy."

Blumenthal nodded his head slowly. He shook Schmidt's hand, as though signaling a peace pact between two great armies. Then he turned, took the elevator back to the hotel lobby, and triumphantly walked through it while nobody got in his way.

He didn't stop until he reached the men's room, where he paid a warm, sentimental visit.

And this time, nobody showed up to arrest him.

FEBRUARY 21, 1979

LIVING ON THE EDGE

The four of them are sitting on the front steps of a deserted apartment building at Monument and Howard Streets at midnight, drinking Thunderbird wine out of paper cups and wondering how to survive the darkness one more time.

They're society's leftovers, three men and a woman, all around 30, living on the fringes of civilization and the edges of our consciousness, scrounging for a place to sleep each night and carrying the contents of their lives in plastic bags.

"Look for an empty apartment," one of them says. "Wherever I find it, that's where I'll sleep."

The three men are quiet and philosophical about their plight, but the woman is not. She's a shriek in motion, a cadaverous thing in T-shirt and golf cap and jeans, strutting and prancing along Monument Street, the wine loosening all the demons inside her. Let the others take their predicament calmly. She wants to rage against the night.

"How come," one of the men starts to say, "this country's got money for Saudi Arabia and not for the people in our own cities? How come . . . ?"

The rest of his words are drowned out by the woman, whose shrill cries split the air. Some of her words are decipherable, most are not.

"Shut up, girl," one of the men tells her.

"Shut up your own self!" she screams back.

The men roll their eyes at her. There is dignity even among the homeless, they're trying to say. They wish to conduct a seminar on their plight, and this bag of bones is making them look bad.

"The country's turning its back on black people," one of the men says. "Like this Bush, see . . . "

"Black people?" the woman cries now. "Black people? Man, ain't no black people no more! Ain't no black people! We ain't black, we're hungry! We're just hungry, and that's the only thing that matters."

The words all seem to come spilling out of her in capital letters. Exclamation marks seem to fly through the night air. She's got her face right up against one man's nose now, letting all her hostilities out in the wrong place.

"You better back off," he warns her.

From behind her, one of the men reaches an arm now and puts his hand over the woman's mouth and drags her backward. But she's all bones, all hard edges, and he's struggling to get his grip.

"My sister," he explains. He says they've been homeless for more than a year. He says he's looked for work, but no employer wants a man with a prison record.

"You know how we got through last winter?" one of the men asks now. "Steam heat."

"Steam heat?"

"Coming out of the sewer," he says softly. "You get cold enough, you'll take heat wherever you find it, it don't matter."

They've all been to the soup kitchens and stood in line for food. Been to city shelters, which struggle against tight budgets to stay open in the warmer months. Even in the shelters, there are unexpected problems.

"Homeless people hurt homeless people," the woman cries now. She's got her cup of Thunderbird in one hand, waving it about as she marches around the sidewalk. "Homeless people stealing from other homeless."

"She's right about that," one of the men says.

"There's a tension," another says. "You definitely get on each other's nerves."

The woman's not placated by having them agree with her. She's off on other flights of attack, again thrusting her face into a man's.

"Back off," he tells her angrily, nearly rising from his seat on cement steps.

"Back off?"

"Back off," he warns again.

"Back off?"

And suddenly the man throws a short left hook into her jaw. She never sees it coming. She staggers back as though struck by lightning, her wine spilling in one direction, her scrawny body in another. The man bolts to his feet. The woman regains her balance and charges at him. Punches are thrown back and forth. Now comes her brother, pulling her back and sticking a long arm into the chest of the other man.

"That ain't the way to treat a lady," the brother says. "I don't care what happened."

The sister, still windmilling her arms around, still screaming, struggles to get in another punch. Then, calm. A police car pulls up, lights flashing. Everybody freezes. All chat amiably for a few moments, trying to cool the air. The scene is no aberration for the cops, who deal with society's leftovers every night.

The city has thousands of them. The woman is right: There are no black people or white people out here, just desperate people. A single hungry or homeless person is a tragedy. A thousand are merely a statistic. The sheer arithmetic numbs us: If so many are out there, we imagine it can't be so bad. Or we turn away, having heard too much.

From Monument Street, two men grab their belongings and begin walking toward Mount Vernon Place. The third man and his sister head toward Howard Street, turn the corner, and disappear.

A moment later, though, you can hear the woman's voice again, hollering at one more demon. It sounds like a cry from the grave.

MAY 5, 1991

BOULEVARD OF INTERRUPTED DREAMS

The fat man stands by the front door of the Pimlico pawn shop with a pistol sticking ostentatiously out of a front pants pocket.

"I want them to know I've got it," he says. He nods toward a couple of guys standing in the doorway, huddled by the window, trying to stay out of a slashing rain on Park Heights Avenue.

Along the street now, they stand in doorways everywhere: At Leon's Pig Pen and the Birdland music store, where electronic sounds curdle into the street; at Willie Richardson's Liquors and Knight's Bar, and at Beeli's Drugs at the corner of Belvedere and Park Heights, where two guys with bottles are holding each other up like beginning ice skaters with weak ankles.

"Do you need the gun?" a guy inside the pawn shop asks the fat man.

"It's a poor neighborhood," he says, as if that explains things. "Super poor. This is the poor man's Hecht Company. They've got their security guards. I've got my gun. And I've got my shotgun."

Through the front window, you see untended kids dart up the sidewalk in cut-off pants and sneakers, trying to duck between the scattery raindrops. One kid stumbles behind, glasses askew, trying hopelessly to keep up with the greyhounds.

Along the walls inside the pawn shop is the stuff of interrupted dreams: rows of guitars and drums, watches and rings, TV sets and radios.

"End of the month," somebody says ruefully, carrying in a monster transistor radio. "Gotta keep it going till the first."

A legion of people has come into the shop now, bearing bits of tinsel to trade in and tide them over for a while. A TV set sitting on a shelf has been turned on, tuned to some network game show where people fight for their own pieces of tinsel. In the pawn shop, a guy holds a stereo outfit in front of the fat man but has no proof at all that it really belongs to him.

This is a tricky business: How do you know, when someone comes in from the street, that the merchandise hasn't been stolen?

"Where's your ID?" the fat man asks.

"Oh, man," the guy with the stereo says. He runs his hands through his pockets in a charade of a search, and rolls his eyes until they vanish into his head.

Now a tall, bony kid, his body shambling into the store in installments, comes in with a gold necklace. The fat man looks at it, throws up his hands. "Take it somewhere else," he says. The tall kid doesn't bother debating. He turns quickly and walks into the dreary afternoon from which he came.

On the street, the rain streaks down out of a sullen sky. A woman races up the block in a soft summer dress, but the rain has plastered the material onto her body now, so that every inch of her underclothing shines through, and the woman laughs and throws her arms around herself in a parody of self-protection, and in the doorways of the pawn shop and Birdland Music and Knight's Bar, the guys whistle and laugh and slap palms, all of it a brief moment of giddiness in the darkness of Park Heights Avenue.

All of this is a stone's throw from the Pimlico Hotel, but it might as well be the other side of the moon.

The people who go to the Pimlico don't hock their jewels to stay afloat until the next welfare check. They don't stand in doorways with paper bags wrapped around whiskey bottles. The people at the Pimlico are high achievers, socially nimble. Many of them once lived in this neighborhood, made a little money, moved out to the greenery of suburbia.

But for years they've returned to this restaurant—not only for its marvelous food, but also to see and be seen, to catch up on local fashion, and to cement a few business deals.

The restaurant seems almost to have been superimposed on the decaying streets—except that it was here long before these streets began to decay and has stayed, against all odds, even as most of the streets around it began to go to hell.

This is the way it sometimes happens around here: Parts of neighborhoods begin to die, and parts begin to hold their breath. Inside their heads, people begin to pack their bags. Somebody checks the real estate ads, and wonders about putting up a sign on the front lawn without panicking the neighbors. It happened this way in Baltimore for a long, shaky time from the late '50s to the late '70s, slowed only when housing prices became too high or there was no one left with money to move away.

"This neighborhood?" Henry Diggs Jr. says now. He's standing behind a counter at Beeli's drugstore, where he's worked the past 11 years.

"Oh, it's deteriorated," he says. "People work the streets in broad daylight. First of the month, they line up out there and wait for people with food stamps in their hand, and they grab 'em. Grab 'em in broad daylight. A lot of them are kids, too."

"Right, kids," says a woman who works in the store. "They scoot in the front door, grab ice cream, and scoot right out. Little kids. But there's adults, too. Not just stealing, but begging. You know, 'You got a quarter, you got 50 cents?' For 18 years, I worked up the street at the Derby Bar, and I knew this woman from there. She came up to me this morning on the street. She said, 'Could you lend me 50 cents till the end of the month?' She didn't have no money."

The inside of the drugstore, like those all over this city, is almost all glass enclosed. Walk in and sense a siege mentality. A stone's throw away, at the glittery Pimlico Hotel, they have a sense of that. The high rollers come in and eat like royalty, surrounded by photographs of famous people.

But they have a parking lot that resembles a stockade. There are sophisticated security precautions. The owners have dreams of moving, because their customers talk about the dangers of this neighborhood where they once lived, but have long since moved away.

And just down the street in a pawn shop, the fat man stands with a gun in his pants pocket, and men huddle in doorways, trying to stay out of the rain.

JULY 14, 1982

REISTERSTOWN ROAD IMMORTALS

At Miller's Deli on Reisterstown Road, somewhere between the uniformed police who have stopped in for coffee and a couple of bookmakers momentarily trying to make themselves look like citizens, we have the immortal Danny Sheelds and the legendary Haircut Jones.

How immortal is Sheelds? Thirty years after the fact, somebody's brought in a photograph of an old billboard near Belvedere Avenue that once declared: "Elect Danny Sheelds."

"Elect him to what?" a guy asks.

"What's the difference?" says Sheelds, the once-and-perhaps-future radio voice who never in his life ran for political office and never would. "Just elect me."

How legendary is Haircut? Nearly half a century after the fact, people who don't even know his actual name still remember him as:

> a. One of the finest door-to-door linoleum salesmen of our troubled century, who turned the whispered phrase "Could you use it?" into a calling card.
> b. The first man to finance a flight from California to Baltimore out of penny deposits on soda bottles.
> c. The former road manager for a young comedy team by the name of Dean Martin and Jerry Lewis.

The two of them, Sheelds and Haircut, turn the business of hanging out into a local art form. Sheelds is temporarily between radio jobs, the last one ending approximately 22 years ago.

Haircut is back in his hometown for a few days, having dropped in from either New York or Las Vegas, he's a little unclear. He's seeing old friends, waiting for post time at Pimlico, and catching up on people like Fat Herby, Abe the Conk, The Mole, and Eats.

"Eats has had heart attack after heart attack, hasn't he?" says Haircut.

"It's his hobby," explains Sheelds.

"What about The Mole?" says Haircut.

A long time ago, The Mole took a bet that he couldn't break a wall. The bet was for 75 cents. Not so much money, except that The Mole hated to lose bets, which is why he drove his car into a wall to win this particular wager.

"He and I were a team," Haircut says proudly.

What we have here are outlines of a life style ad-libbed across the decades, beginning during the Depression, when people hustled and rolled the dice with their lives and never quite got over it.

Thus, the notion of "hanging out" has come into a certain disrepute. It has nothing to do with killing time, merely with marking it, with a certain honorable checking of the angles until something profitable comes along.

Miller's Deli, for example, is legendary for such practice. It was here that the immortal Nookie the Bookie, known to bettors as Nookie Brown and to God as Daniel Brozowsky, set a record that is still believed to be intact in the annals of criminal justice, which goes like this:

The police knew that a certain small percentage of hanging out involved activities frowned upon by law—making book, for example. So the cops had a guy across the street from Miller's, spying from the roof of the old Stewart's Department Store at Reisterstown Road Plaza.

The cop looked through his binoculars and noticed somebody hand Nookie something wrapped in paper. It was believed to be bets. The cops then leaped into action. It was the only time in history somebody was grabbed for possession of strudel.

"Yeah, Nookie," somebody says now.

"Nookie knew about life," Haircut Jones says, suddenly getting philosophical. "Everything had to do with scuffling, and with beating the check."

"That was the common denominator," says Sheelds. "No money."

Some guys would sell shopping bags on Lexington Street for a nickel apiece. Another guy wrote bad checks for a living. At Christmas one year, everybody gave him pens. One fellow worked as a towel boy in a house of ill repute, so he'd have a place to sleep.

By the late '40s, Sheelds was working local radio. Years before it became a radio staple, he was doing two-way talk. Electronically, it was crude. Nobody had the equipment to pick up the caller's voice, so Danny would listen and repeat what the caller was saying virtually as the words were coming over the wires. The alternative was silence over the airwaves, and listeners tuning out. So Sheelds became one of those people who can keep talking without coming up for air.

Meanwhile, Haircut was working as a tap dancer on roller skates at the old Picadilly Club on Fayette Street. He'd get his meals next door at Klein's Pool Room where, if you didn't have enough money, you could buy a piece of a sandwich.

Then Haircut got lucky. At the old Chanticleer Night Club on Charles Street one evening maybe 40 years ago, there was a young comic duo, Martin and Lewis. They needed a road manager. Haircut, mindful of his roller-skating career, mentioned he had show business background, carefully leaving out the part that he was currently hustling linoleum door to door. Next thing he knew, he was working for the comics.

Something always comes along. It's the knack of hanging out. Miller's is a fine place for it, but the great ones, the guys like Sheelds and Haircut, can do it anywhere. With them, it's an art form.

JUNE 14, 1990

THE BENCHES OF EASTERN AVENUE

In the summer of his 94th year, Alfred G. "Whitey" Mansberger prowls the corner of Eastern Avenue and Conkling Street with his fist in a clinch and his mind inclined toward punching somebody in the nose.

"Look around," he says, waving an arm expansively. "This is pitiful. You got people everywhere, but you got no place for them to stop and talk to each other."

With the late-morning temperature already up around 90, and trucks belching exhaust fumes into the muggy East Baltimore air, Whitey's a picture to behold: white straw hat, white shoes, powder-blue shirt and pants, white tie, angry attitude.

"Am I right?" he says. He says this to everybody. He says it to friends, and he says it to neighbors walking along Eastern Avenue, and he says it to Evelyn Waire, 73 years old, as she turns the corner from Eastern to Conkling with packages filling her arms.

"Of course you're right," she says. "What are we talking about?"

She looks around for a little help, which we will give her in a minute. But first, a message from Evelyn—on behalf of the telephone company, but mainly on behalf of East Baltimore tradition.

"They called me the other night," Evelyn tells Whitey.

"The phone company?" he says.

"Yeah," she says. "They wanted me to subscribe to some low-cost long-distance program. I said I wasn't interested. They asked me if I made a lot of long-distance calls. I said I have three grandchildren who live out of town."

"That's long distance," says Whitey.

"Yeah," agrees Evelyn, "but I told 'em, 'Hon, my grandchildren call me on their own money. And anyway, I don't make long-distance calls. I'm from Highlandtown. I need my bingo money.' "

At Eastern and Conkling, Whitey and Evelyn share a laugh over this. The laughter, and the idle chatter, and the friendships that linger through the years, happen to be the bone of Whitey's contention.

If a community is more than a loose collection of people, then where are people supposed to collect? If neighborhoods are places where people share more than mere geography, then how do we make the geography livable?

There used to be benches at Eastern and Conkling. Some time back, the city did something very nice. They made little miniparks on each of the four corners at this intersection, laying in red brick where there was cement, planting shade trees, and putting three or four benches on each corner.

The benches became gathering places for people, most of them elderly, many of whom would shop along this commercial strip of Eastern Avenue and then grab a soda and sit to talk with friends before heading home.

Several months ago, though, the city took away the benches. Several community merchants said the benches were attracting the wrong kind of people: street drunks, to be exact, who'd sometimes sleep on the benches.

Some of these merchants told city hall: Get these benches out of here. Some residents said: Don't you dare move them. City hall listened to the merchants.

"And so," Whitey Mansberger is saying now, "we got no place to sit down here any more. You know what that means? We got more elderly people in Highlandtown than anywhere in the city, and they got nowhere to rest. They come up here to shop, they pay money, and they want to sit and talk for a while. It could be your mother. It could be my mother. What are they supposed to do, lean on a wall?"

Now Whitey begins corralling people again, some of them friends, some of them strangers, most of them elderly, all of them absolutely on his side.

Highlandtown has always had a strong sense of street culture, of people sitting on front steps, of parents sending kids down to the corner grocery store for a snowball and a pack of cigarettes, of families strolling the shops of Eastern Avenue.

In minutes at Eastern and Conkling, on a day for which God specifically invented air conditioning, you still have people stopping to chat about last week's Fourth of July fireworks at Patterson Park, about the city's housing department, about the Orioles, about the cost of steamed crabs.

But then everybody moves quickly away. There's no place to sit and stretch out the conversation a bit.

And this is why Whitey Mansberger, in the prime of his 94th year, is prowling the street in his straw hat and looking as if he wants to hit somebody, a politician most likely, but any villain will do.

"I worked in the steel mill at Sparrows Point all my life," he said. "No job is harder or hotter. But I'll tell you, this has got me hotter than anything. These are my people who came here, and now we can't come here any more."

And if that doesn't mean anything to the life of a city, then what does?

JULY 12, 1990

THE ROMANTIC ASPECTS OF SNOW: ROGERS AVENUE

With snow spilling out of the sky above Rogers Avenue, she says to him, "Let's go for a walk."

He is watching the 27th rerun of a situation comedy in which the laugh track drowns out much of the dialogue, and he's trying to pick up punch lines he missed the first 26 times he watched this same show.

"It's snowing out there," he says dismissively.

"I know it's snowing," she says. "It'll be fun."

"It's also dark out there," he says.

"I'll hold your hand."

On Rogers Avenue, they walk under a canopy of branches and look up at the snow drifting past street lamps. They haven't done anything like this in years, just walking for the sake of walking, just feeling the elements around them, just reintroducing themselves to each other with nobody else around.

"Listen to the silence," she says.

"I forgot it could be this quiet," he says. "I think every bird caught the last flight to Miami."

He feels a little self-conscious. They are married people with children, and he feels like some miscast actor tabbed to play the lead in a Pepsi Generation commercial.

In the snow and the silence, he feels something ancient and half-forgotten stirring in his bones, but he is certain someone will spot the two of them from a warm living room and holler at them to get inside on such a night as this.

She slips her hand into his. He wants to steal a look at her face but feels a little silly about it. She puts her arm around his waist, and reflexively he puts his arm around hers.

"I think this is where you're supposed to kiss me like Bogey would," she says. The reference frees him a little. Bogey was middle aged; he's middle aged, too. It's okay to be holding hands on a snowy night and not be 22 years old.

He leans down and kisses her curly head and then tilts her chin upward, when a pile of snow, giving in to gravity, suddenly plummets from overhead branches and lands on them.

"Nature's wondrous sense of timing," she laughs.

He begins to jump about, partly to get the snow out of his collar and partly just to be jumping about. The movement seems to shake something loose in his soul.

"Come on," he says, and on Rogers Avenue now, the two of them begin running and swirling and losing their breath and they land in some forgotten place of the heart about 1962.

He begins to sing: "The Jets are gonna have their way / Tonight."

She sings: "Some enchanted evening / You may see a stranger."

He sings: "I have often walked / Down this street before / But the pavement always stayed / Beneath my feet before."

She sings: "Frère Jacques / Frère Jacques."

" 'Frère Jacques?' " he cries half-mockingly, and then she launches into an old Girl Scout song, the words only partly forgotten, and now the transformation to youth is complete, and the two of them stand in the street and hug each other, and he notices nobody is hollering from doorways for the two of them to get inside.

The world belongs to them. A street lamp puts them in the center of the universe. They are alone under this perfect canopy of branches, and he kisses her again, and they pull apart and look at each other delightedly, and then they kiss again.

He feels the night air moving through his chest. She is wearing a knit sweater beneath her overcoat, and he reaches in and warms his hands on her sides. They look at each other and smile silly little smiles and seem to be discovering people they misplaced somewhere along the way.

"I love you," he admits, "more than I love watching television reruns."

"I love you," she admits, "more than I love the Sunday *Times* crossword puzzle."

This is getting into very serious business.

"I love you," he says, "more than 'Doonesbury.' "

"I love you more than Elvis singing 'Love Me Tender.' "

"I love you," he says, getting into truly meaningful stuff now, "more than I love playing basketball at the gym."

"I love you more than our electric blanket."

"More than that?" he asks.

"Yes."

"Then you do love me, don't you?"

Such a thought doesn't always occur to either of them. They love each other for a few minutes, here and there, but then it blows away. Over the years, it's just a given, like breathing, but it's not a thing they stop and think about a lot.

They walk along a little farther. He reaches down and makes a snowball and throws it as far as he can. She puts her hands against her heart in a comic schoolgirl swoon.

He reaches for her hands and says: "Would you take me again to be your lawfully wedded husband, through sickness and health, through arthritis and snoring?"

"Would you take me again through varicose veins and carry-in dinners?"

"I will if you will."

And the two of them smile at each other in the snow on Rogers Avenue, and the branches above bend over them, and from where they stand it almost looks like a wedding canopy created by God.

DECEMBER 17, 1989

LOU KARPOUZIE: THE LEGEND OF NORTH KANE STREET

Some guys create a legend in their youth and live off the residuals the rest of their lives. Not Lou Karpouzie, who keeps building on his. All the glory of his high school days, the touchdowns and the girls gathered around him, is nothing like the gifts he's given back in the last half-century.

You want to talk legend? Back at Patterson High School, back in the war years, back when the football team was winning the public school championship and forming the powerhouse clubs that would win 29 games in a row, it was Karpouzie who took Patterson into the big game against City College, whom Patterson never had beaten.

Only it didn't look like Karpouzie would play. A couple of days before the game, his father died. You have to play, his mother said. Dad would want it. Lou scored the winning touchdown.

"Memorable days," Karpouzie was saying the other day, over lunch at Sabatino's. He had a gleam in his eyes shining back maybe 50 years. "You know, playing football, you had girls around all the time. I tell you, those girls, they used to do my homework for me."

He never wanted to let those days get away. For years, he's been manager of the city's Department of Special Events, but he's spent his off-hours over in East Baltimore, holding things together, looking out for people.

Like Thanksgiving Day. For the past 14 years, he's had holiday dinners at Patterson High's cafeteria, where about five hundred of the community's elderly and poor drop in for a meal.

Or the scholarship he set up for a graduating senior at Patterson who's got outstanding grades but needs help with college money. Or the way he took an old landfill near the school on North Kane Street and turned it into two ball fields, which are used by roughly five thousand kids every year. Five years ago, the city named the fields after Lou.

Then there are the athletic leagues he's organized for kids, and the wheelchair basketball games, and the reunions he's put together every year for the old-time athletes from Patterson, with profits going back to the high school.

"This sort of stuff," he was saying, "keeps people together. It brings communities together, it makes them stronger. I like to see people happy. If they're happy, I'm happy."

Naturally, this doesn't mean every event is universal bliss. Karpouzie remembers coaching one of his 14- to 16-year-old teams, sponsored by Butta Brothers. They played a club out of Dundalk, at the old White Swann Field at Oldham and Lombard, which is now a truck stop.

A slight fight broke out, involving maybe everybody in sight—players, spectators, referees. By the time the cops arrived, the Dundalk kids were huddled on their bus, and the Highlandtown kids were commencing to turn it upside down.

Or the neighborhood dances at Unity Hall on Dundalk Avenue. Every week, Lou would rent spiffy tuxedos from Stanley Hiken's place for some of the bigger kids to wear, identifying them as chaperones.

One time a fight breaks out. It starts inside the hall, and it works its way onto Dundalk Avenue, where it stops all traffic. The guys in the tuxedos are trying to break it up, and their outfits are getting torn asunder at the elbows and knees.

On Monday, Karpouzie takes the tuxes back to Stanley Hiken, who looks them over.

"These tuxedos," he says. "Did they look like this when you rented 'em from me?"

"Oh, yeah," says Karpouzie.

"OK," says Hiken, "no problem. 'Cause I'm gonna rent you the same ones every week."

For maybe 30 years, Karpouzie was one of the great dance promoters around town, not only at Unity Hall but at the old Dixie Ballroom at Gwynn Oak Park. He brought in Ray Charles, Smokey Robinson and the Miracles, James Brown, the Shirelles, Frankie Avalon.

"Yeah, Frankie Avalon," Karpouzie said. "His father ran a hall up in Philly. I went to see him. I said, 'I'd love to get Frankie down to Baltimore, but I can't afford him.' You know, he was very big at the time.

"The father says, 'Tell him I said he should go.' He came down here for $400. He walked into Unity Hall, the girls grabbed him by his ankles and lifted him up."

Now, though, Karpouzie's focusing on two things: Thanksgiving dinner, and a Patterson reunion at Steelworkers Hall, which he's organizing with old neighborhood guys Edward Katrinic, Bernie Weber, Gus Janouris, and Gus Hansen.

"I just get a good feeling when I see people enjoying themselves," Karpouzie said. "Like, one time we had this school reunion, and I look across the room and there's this nun there. She's smiling at me, and she says, 'You don't recognize me, do you?' "

"I said, 'No, sister, I don't.' "

"She said, 'You should. I used to do your homework for you.' "

OCTOBER 23, 1994

POLITICOS

The Not-Ready-for-Prime-Time

Politicians

The Not-Ready-for-Prime-Time Politicians are a thing of beauty and a joy occasionally. The title is meant to give them a certain cockeyed respect: These people aren't bland enough for prime time. They're not sneaky enough to be big time.

Too many politicians today have learned to conduct themselves like television anchors, or accountants. They've got the diction about right, and somebody's taught them how to dress appropriately, and they think this passes for brilliance.

My favorite politicians are those who never learned to disguise their flaws. Take, for example, a guy like George Santoni, the one-time state delegate. I visited him at Lewisburg Federal Penitentiary, after he went there on extortion charges. "You know what I'd really like to do when I get out?" he said, resting his meaty hands across his midsection. "I'd like the mayor to send me down to Annapolis and let me be the lobbyist for the city."

He wanted to mix with the old legislative crowd, and use the gifts of persuasion once considered remarkable by politicians as well as by federal prosecutors. "But I guess that might be a little awkward for the mayor," he said. "I mean, me with a record for extortion, trying to get money for the city." He paused thoughtfully, shrugged his big shoulders, and brightened. "On the other hand," he said, "who better than an extortionist?"

I like the chutzpah. I like somebody saying, OK, I made a mistake, now let's move on from here. I like the politicians who don't rearrange their feistiest stuff for the prime-time crowds.

Take Ross Pierpont. Here's a man who was chief of surgery at Maryland General Hospital for many years, but it was never enough. He ran for every political office he could find. And lost every time, but kept trying.

Once, he ran for Congress out in Harford County, even though he lived in the city. He figured his medical office counted as a personal address. His opponents said otherwise. One of them challenged him: "Do you even know the people here?"

"Know them?" the surgeon-candidate replied. "I've had my hands inside most of them."

This made him unready for prime time, but always good for an invigorating time.

THE BEST MAYOR IN AMERICA

On a night when William Donald Schaefer should be dancing with the gods, he looks as if his world is falling apart.

He's standing in a little alcove at Lexington Market two nights ago, with the bright lights and the merriment of the 15th annual City Fair just outside the door, a father figure hovering over his children at play.

Nobody notices him. The mayor's hands are jammed into his pockets, his shoulders are slouched, his head bowed. It should be a grand moment of triumph, but in his head is the sense of national humiliation.

The mayor of Baltimore is the most forlorn of figures. He's just dined royally at Mercado, the continental restaurant, with his lady friend Hilda Mae Snoops. *Esquire* magazine has just named him the best mayor in America. The City Fair, his symbol of Baltimore's life after obituaries, is blossoming right outside this door.

And yet Schaefer has the look of a man stepping onto the ledge of a very tall building.

It's the *Esquire* piece. There's a warm light shining into the alcove, but Schaefer doesn't feel it. People are dancing happily on the parking lot outside, but Schaefer doesn't see them. Friends are offering consolation to him, and the mayor of Baltimore doesn't hear them.

"You don't understand it," he says. "That piece was just devastating. And everybody in the whole country is gonna read it."

This isn't just a momentary concern. At noon, at Charles Center, he was calling the magazine article "the worst piece of journalism in history," sputtering the words out of his mouth.

"But it calls you the best mayor in America," said a startled man who hadn't yet read the piece.

"Have you seen it?" asked Schaefer, eyes blazing. "They talked about my mother's funeral. Now why did they have to write about a thing like that?"

The blaze in his eyes was turning into a blur now. He took a deep breath and looked for somebody else to talk to, some change of subject, something to clear the emotions out of the air, when an aide walked up and the mayor turned and walked away.

"He's upset," said the aide, "over the funeral scene, and the description of him crying there. And the descriptions of the mayor cursing. And the inference that the mayor has no real friends."

The last is puzzling. One always thought the mayor was intending friendlessness as his personal image: the soul so dedicated to saving his city, to filling every last pot hole, that he had no time, no inclination, no energy left at the end of each exhausting day for ordinary friends.

But now that someone has speculated such a thing in public, the mayor's wounded. He doesn't seem aware that such a picture is wildly flattering, the image of a totally selfless urban saint.

There's more to it than that, though. We're talking about a very sensitive man here, and there are random descriptions in the *Esquire* piece that would hurt the most thick-skinned human being.

Nobody, even in the course of being called the "best damned mayor in America," wants to be dubbed "The Great Melon Head."

Nobody wants sexual allegations dug up from beyond the grave.

"Friends, money, women: he didn't seem to want to have any," Richard Ben Cramer writes in *Esquire*. "Lots of guys would go down to The Block after council. Not Schaefer. Never liked girls. Dominic Leone from the Sixth District, he'd offer a hundred dollars to an apple that Schaefer was gay. But Dom didn't know anything. No one did. Schaefer lived at home with his mother." Unfair.

Schaefer's people are passing the Leone remark off as a joke, when in fact it wasn't. Leone believed it, but for the dumbest of reasons. He came from that line of men—and it crosses all generations, all ethnic origins, all classes—who need to flex their masculinity for the boys, need to advertise their sexual conquests, real and imagined.

Anybody who knew Leone, or knows Schaefer, knows the remark was based on empty locker-room posturing, and nothing else. And Leone, eight years after his death, isn't around to change his remarks.

In fact, though, the mayor generally ought to be thrilled about the magazine article. It captures a man who doesn't merely love his city, but whose heart throbs in perfect communion with the city's own.

He doesn't like the scenes of him cursing at his staff? Piffle. The cursing, the random browbeating, show a man utterly driven to make his people understand their calling.

"Why can't they see? So little time . . ." Cramer writes.

Don Schaefer is a man who long ago melted his entire ego into the city's own. He lost track of his own personality, maybe intentionally. Maybe there were things he wanted to leave behind.

The *Esquire* piece brings a few of them back to life. Just when the mayor thought he'd buried his own ego, he found out he hadn't. Just when he assumed his entire persona was wrapped around the town, he found out there are pieces of himself that still breathe.

SEPTEMBER 20, 1984

MFUME'S OLD NEIGHBORHOOD

From Robert and Division Streets, where he grew up in West Baltimore, Rep. Kweisi Mfume turns his car down an alley and sees this crippled old man walking through the frigid, scattery raindrops.

"Bop," the congressman cries, lowering his car window. "Hey, Bop."

The old man looks up from a metal walker he's leaning on for support. His eyes take a moment to focus, and then they light up. Immediately, the two men enter a comfort zone, with talk of old times, treasured hangouts, missing friends.

"It's good to see you," the old man says. The congressman nods his head. Bop appreciatively looks over Mfume's car, eyes his fresh suit of clothes. "Listen," he says, not quite choking on sentiment. "Could I have a dollar?"

"Huh?"

"I'm not going to the liquor store with it," he assures, though no one has asked.

Mfume reaches into his pocket, pulls out some money, hands it to his old friend. He holds the man's hand, and then holds it a little longer. The old man moves away then, leaning on his walker, and Mfume slowly puts his car into gear.

"Ol' Bop," he says after a few silent moments. He sighs. "You know something? He's 15 years younger than me. He's 29 years old."

In Mfume's old neighborhood, people sometimes age in terrible ways. So has the neighborhood. In a cold drizzle, Mfume gets out of his car on Division Street and points out remembrances of things past: Over here was a grocery store, now boarded up; over there a tuxedo rental shop, grown over with weeds now, burned out in the riots of nearly a quarter-century ago and ignored ever since; a few doors away, the row house where Mfume lived his adolescent years until one night his mother died right there in his arms.

"It was me and my three younger sisters," he remembers. "There was no money. The gas and electric was always getting turned off, and we'd pull down the curtains so people couldn't see we were using candles. And then, the night my mother died, I felt absolutely, totally out in the world, paying a price I didn't understand. They sent my sisters to my grandmother, and me to my uncles. And I felt all alone."

Two weeks later, he dropped out of high school, took on odd jobs, shined shoes, sold produce, shoveled snow. Began seeing girls, and began to father children. Five of them, all boys, arrived in four years. Mfume never married any of their mothers, and never told voters during his city council campaigns.

"I grew up in a tough, tough neighborhood," he says ruefully, still seeming a little dazed all these years later. "This was a typical problem there. And it seemed like every time I did it, I got hit. Another baby. Everybody else was sliding through, and I wasn't.

"I realized I had a choice to make. I could be a responsible father, or do what a lot of other guys in my neighborhood did: push for abortions or just get lost. But I didn't. I've always felt driven to be there for my kids. From the beginning, they've all known each other as brothers, and I'm their father."

When he ran for Congress the first time, and his opponent broke the news about his out-of-wedlock children, Mfume produced affidavits from his sons, lauding him as a father. Mfume humbly called himself "an imperfect man" and found himself elected to the U.S. Congress despite his imperfections.

Now in his fresh suit of clothes and his big car, he seems to have arrived in his old neighborhood from some other world, but not so he'd want to stress it. This is still psychological home. In Washington, Mfume has been voted head of the Congressional Black Caucus, but all political instincts still flow from here, or else the lessons of his life count for nothing.

DECEMBER 13, 1992

OSWALD PAROLED?

A telephone call arrives the other day from the Baltimore City Courthouse, from one of our high-ranking government officials, who is theatrically upset and shall go nameless here so as not to lose all public stature.

"Are you aware what's happening?" this official asks.

"What's that?" I ask.

"Lee Harvey Oswald," the official says. "He's been paroled from prison." This, I didn't think was possible. And I don't respond immediately, because my mind has slipped out of gear, as I frantically consider which one of us has been misreading a certain catastrophic moment in American history for the past 19 years.

"Are you there?" the official asks.

"Oswald?" I say hesitantly. "The guy who shot Kennedy?"

"Right," the official says. "He's been paroled from the lockup at Fort Meade."

"Oswald," I say, "who shot John Kennedy? You're not thinking of Sirhan Sirhan, are you? The guy who shot Bobby Kennedy? Or James Earl Ray, who shot Martin Luther King?"

Or John Wilkes Booth, I might have added, but didn't.

"No," the official says. "Lee Harvey Oswald."

And so my mind is swimming. I'm dealing with an authority figure here, who's in a position to know Important Things, while I'm an ordinary citizen who has, frankly, not been getting enough sleep lately. So I have a decision to make: Do I tell the official what I believe to be the facts of the case—that Oswald, the apparent assassin of President Kennedy nearly 19 years ago, was himself shot to death two days later and is therefore, at the very least, not likely to be paroled from anything?

Or do I, in the process, run the risk of letting it out that I've misinterpreted the story all these years, when every other person in America has not?

I decide to take a chance.

"Lee Harvey Oswald," I declare, trying to sound as confident as possible, "is dead."

And now comes a pause on the line, a silence that lasts several seconds and ends with the voice of this highly respected official, this Important Person, this adult, asking: "Are you sure?"

"Yes," I say. "He was being transferred from one lockup to another by the Dallas police, and a man named Jack Ruby shot him and killed him."

"Lee Harvey Oswald?" the official says incredulously.

"Yes," I say. "Listen, where did you get your information?"

"It just came in the mail," the official says. "It's in the National District Attorneys Association Newsletter."

Now I'm getting worried. I know the mail is slow, but not quite this slow. And I'm thinking, either I've been living under a serious delusion for the past two decades, or I've just been handed one of the greatest scoops in the history of news, and I wonder if it's too late to alert the Warren Commission.

"Let me ask you this," I say. "On top of the article, does it say anything like, 'This is a hypothetical scenario, in the event Oswald had lived?' "

"No," the official says.

"Do me a favor," I say. "Send me a copy of this article. I could be sitting on one of the great stories of our time."

All of this took place on Wednesday. By Friday, I still hadn't received the District Attorneys Association Newsletter and, not feeling too confident about speedy mail delivery, I dropped by the courthouse office of this official.

"You got me," the official says right away.

"What do you mean?" I say.

"Oswald's dead," the official admits. "Two people heard me talking to you on the phone and confirmed it for me."

"Oh, good," I say, "because I wasn't sure if I was losing my mind. I mean, I can still remember standing there with my father when Jack Ruby came out with the gun, and we saw the whole thing happen on television."

And here is the thing this official said to me, which is so good that I wrote it down right away so I could repeat it for you now: "See, that's my problem. I never watch television."

"But it was in all the papers," I reply.

"Well," the official says, "I just sat here reading the article about Oswald being paroled, and I thought, 'My God, they've done it again. They've let another madman go free.' "

Next question: Where does the National District Attorneys Association come off publishing such an article? Jack Yelverton, executive director, explains it was written by Professor Carl Bode, in the aftermath of the John Hinckley decision in the shooting of President Reagan. It offers a possible scenario of what might have happened had Oswald lived, been sent to prison, and later been eligible for parole.

"Maybe," says Yelverton, stifling a chuckle, "we should run a disclaimer. Out of fairness to whomever might have misunderstood the article."

"So," I ask, "I can safely inform my readers that Lee Harvey Oswald is still dead?"

"I think you can assume that."

So there it is, folks.

Just remember, you read it here last.

OCTOBER 12, 1982

YOUR CITY COUNCIL ON PRIME-TIME CABLE

If Eddie Fenton were alive today, this would kill him.

Fenton was the WCBM radio reporter who covered Baltimore City Council meetings for about 40 years, frequently sober and always in a state of thinly veiled contempt. The Baltimore City Council meets in ornate splendor and semiconfusion on the fourth floor of City Hall. They meet on Monday nights, ostensibly to discuss public business. Fenton always saw them for what they were: a bunch of lightweights pretending to do meaningful work in public.

On Monday nights at City Hall, when some self-important council member would be posturing at length, the voice of Fenton could be heard, gentle as a grenade going off inside your hat: "Come on, kickoff's at nine o'clock. I got a ballgame to watch, let's go."

He'd have shuddered at last week's announcement that proceedings of the Baltimore City Council will now be televised, gavel to gavel, on Monday nights.

The Not-Ready-for-Prime-Time Politicians will be thrust upon the heretofore innocent and unsuspecting Not-Ready-for-this-Kind-of-Culture-Shock subscribers of cable television's Channel 44.

Is this a great country, or what?

Currently, most council meetings last about an hour. In Cambridge, Massachusetts, where they have already begun a grand experiment in live city council TV coverage, there are now meetings that last up to eight hours.

Naturally, this is because no politician, not even Michael Mitchell, would ever dream of posturing for TV cameras. Somewhere in Lewisburg, Pennsylvania, where he's temporarily residing behind bars, Mitchell must be tearing his hair out at this TV news. In his days as a city council member, Mitchell was always given to the longest and most flowery of orations. He had what council observers always called his Around-the-Beltway speech, where he'd amble, free form, from one topic to another, sometimes veering off through the various centuries of human existence when the subject was merely some local zoning ordinance.

One night, Mitchell spoke at length of the greatness of the American system of democracy. He mentioned the founding fathers. He dropped rose petals around the legacy of James Madison.

At the end of it, Councilman Dominic "Mimi" DiPietro rose and declared formally, "This guy Madison sounds pretty good. Who is he?"

Another time, Mitchell made reference to the 18th-century English statesman Edmund Burke. From across the room came the voice of Eddie Fenton: "Mitchell, you wouldn't know Edmund Burke from Phil Burke."

(For the record, since such things are important, Phil Burke was the wild man owner of a saloon on Maryland Avenue just below North. One night, he attempted to drive off without bothering to close his car door. The door ripped off the car, and Burke kept right on going. An hour later, he called the saloon. "It's starting to rain," he said. "Would somebody please roll up my car window?")

But we digress, which is what the Baltimore City Council does routinely.

Once, before his own prison hiatus, then-council president Wally Orlinsky took certain unnamed members to task for failure to do their homework at committee meetings.

Dr. Emerson Julian, the West Baltimore councilman, leaped to his feet and put his face as close as he could to Orlinsky's. "You ever accuse me again," Julian said, "and I'll drag you down by your hind legs in front of everybody. I don't care. Don't talk about me like that in public."

"You?" said Orlinsky. "You thought I was talking about you?"

"You weren't?"

"No."

"Oh." Julian shrugged his shoulders. "In that case, I have nothing more to say."

The overwhelming percentage of important council business is conducted at committee hearings, where legislation is hammered together. But some—and Michael Mitchell was a classic culprit—rarely attended meetings but almost always showed up on Mondays, ready to speechify at a moment's notice, when he knew the three commercial TV stations would be looking for quick, dramatic sound bites for the evening news.

If there had been gavel-to-gavel coverage in Mitchell's time, they'd have had to turn out the lights at midnight just to get rid of him. But it's not just the Mitchells of the world who are troubling.

It's human instinct, the need to look important when the cameras start to roll and people are watching. Monday night council meetings often consist of ceremonial stuff: introductions of school contest winners, announcements of longtime wedding anniversaries, introductions of various Democratic Central Committee members who stumbled into the room with nothing better to do.

Do council members really want voters to know this is what they do for a living? Or, during the slow moments, will there be some voice-over narrator, speaking in the hushed, reverent tones of a celebrity bowling announcer, playing for time until something important happens?

He'd better show up looking to fill a lot of space.

OCTOBER 30, 1988

CIVICS IN THE AGE OF DOMINIC LEONE

Eight in the morning in the 600 block of East Fort Avenue, in South Baltimore, Dominic Leone Jr. is serving a guy a shot of Seagram's and a Pabst beer from behind the bar at Leone's Cafe.

The front door has been flung open, but the air is heavy in here. Leone, cigarette dangling from a puffy lower lip, has dark hair, a large stomach slowly giving in to gravity, and a tip on a horse that he says cannot lose.

"The horse is running July 4," he says, "and it's hot. Only just don't put his name in the paper, see?"

"That ain't like the last horse you had, is it?" comes a high-pitched voice from the far end of the bar. "That horse is still out there running."

"Whattaya want?" Leone says, feigning hurt. "The horse finished first in the seventh race, didn't it?"

"Yeah," says another voice, "but it was runnin' in the sixth."

Laughter follows, none louder than Leone's. There are maybe 10 people in the bar early this muggy morning, and they're his people. The bar has been his family's for 32 years. He grew up in the apartment above it. This place is home, and these people understand him. In the civics books with which we instruct our children, they never mention the people like Leone, who passes out tips on a horse and simultaneously runs for a seat on the Baltimore City Council.

He wishes to be his father's son.

The father, Dominic Leone Sr., was a Sixth District councilman from 1960 to April 1976, when a deranged man with a gun named Charles Hopkins ran through City Hall spraying bullets. Leone was one of his arbitrary victims.

"Dad said politics was a rough game, a whore's game," the son says. "I don't see it that way. I just know it's in my blood."

The father had a doughy face and a body shaped like a pillow. If you knocked on his City Hall office in the middle of the day, chances are you'd find him kneeling on the floor, with his sleeves rolled up and a Marlboro in his lips, in the middle of a high-level crap game.

He was not eloquent. He did not pretend to have some grand philosophy of life. He led a hectic, Rabelaisian life and sometimes got into trouble for it. But when constituents came to him with problems, he was there, and this got him elected again and again until Charles Hopkins and the gun. The son says his own life turned around that day. He runs for office not only against three incumbents, but against his own history.

"I never robbed or killed anybody," he says, which is a pleasant fact but not quite a campaign slogan. "The only person I hurt was myself, drinking and fighting."

Also, a little gambling. A few years ago, Leone ran for a seat in the state legislature. An opponent began saying nasty things about him. "He's telling people I'm a numbers runner," Leone complained to a reporter he knew.

"But you *are* a numbers runner," the reporter said. Leone thought about this for a moment.

"Yeah," he said finally. "But he don't have to tell people, does he?"

He's a product of these streets, of a certain mind-set that says a young man sows wild oats, and burns things out of his system, and over time learns to take his place in proper society, providing he has survived.

At the heart of this world was the family bar on Fort Avenue, the boisterous center of operations not only for South Baltimore politics but for some incredibly successful amateur baseball teams that produced, among others, major leaguers Reggie Jackson, Al Kaline, Tom Phoebus, Dave Boswell, Willie Aikens, Moose Haas, and Ron Swoboda.

Leone was four when he started working as bat boy for the old Leone's baseball teams. Every year the team would travel to Johnstown, Pennsylvania, for the All-America Amateur Baseball Association championships, which the Leone's team captured with wondrous frequency.

"After a while," Leone says, "I got to know the town real good, and I'd show our players the hot spots. Where the girls were. Plus I took all their money in card games."

He was in elementary school at the time. It's all part of a crazy history, which he says is strictly behind him now. He says this is a new Leone. In the humid early morning air inside the bar, he pours a man a beer and gives him change. Too much change, the man tells him.

"Shows I'm honest," Leone says.

"Shows you're running for office," somebody else says.

JUNE 30, 1983

EAST MEETS WEST AT BUD'S CRAB HOUSE

On Monday, precisely as Ronald Reagan and Mikhail S. Gorbachev took a few small steps toward peace on earth, another, slightly less-publicized but no less monumental summit was taking place in U.S.-Soviet relations.

Yuri Balovlenkov walked to Bud Paolino's crab house on East Lombard Street, and there he met Mimi DiPietro.

International diplomacy may never be the same.

Balovlenkov is the Russian refusenik, the veteran of hunger strikes, the man who stood up to the KGB, the one who fought for nine years to come to America and live with his wife and children in East Baltimore, the man who arrived here 10 days ago and whose story has been told on network television and in national magazines and newspapers.

Mimi is the articulate and highly polished city councilman, the Alistair Cooke of East Baltimore, the man who looks out for anybody in the First District with a voting card who needs help, such as a job. He's the internationally sophisticated statesman who heard Yuri's name last week and forthrightly declared: "Who?"

Mimi is now Yuri's city councilman.

"Who?" Mimi said again, when Yuri's name was repeated to him.

"Who?!" declared a friend of Mimi's when he broke the news to DiPietro the other day. "Who?! Yuri Balovlenkov. The Russian refusenik who's been in the news everywhere. His wife is Elena. You remember her. She's been trying to get him out for nine years. She lives in Highlandtown."

"I don't know her," said Mimi.

"This is a very important guy," said Mimi's friend. "He's an international figure. You could tell him about America."

"I ain't got time to show him America," said Mimi. "Give that to somebody else that's got time. I got a meeting with Mary Pat Clarke in a few minutes."

"No," the friend explained, "I just thought, since he'll live in Highlandtown, maybe you could give him some help if he needs it."

"Oh, sure," said Mimi. "Can we get the Sons of Italy to do anything?"

"Uh, he's Russian."

"He is?" said Mimi. "Oh, I thought he was a dago. What do I know from Russians?"

About as much as Yuri Balovlenkov knows about crabs—which is why, on Monday, precisely as Reagan and Gorbachev were meeting, so were Yuri and Mimi and some friends.

"You the Russian?" asked Mimi, marching into Bud's crab house and looking all the way up at Yuri's gently smiling face.

"Yes," said Yuri, standing next to his wife, Elena. Around a big table sat a dozen Baltimoreans, looking at a sumptuous, riotous spread of steamed crabs and fried shrimp and crab fluffs and steamed shrimp and crab cakes and beer and soda and wine and noise that rang like music.

"Let me look at you," said Mimi, sitting himself down next to Yuri and me. "Are you a tough Russian, or what?"

Yuri smiled, but looked a little confused.

"Do you understand what he's saying?" I asked.

"About half," said Yuri.

"Us, too," I said.

"You're the gentleman from Russia, huh?" said Mimi.

"Yes," Yuri nodded.

"Well, God bless you," said Mimi, and reached for a steamed crab.

Around the table, rich with laughter now, were some who had helped bring about this historic meeting: Richard Sher and Marty Bass, the Channel 13 TV personalities, and Al Isella, the retired East Baltimore bookmaker.

I know what you're thinking.

One week in America, and Yuri's going through this kind of culture shock?

The man will ask for diplomatic immunity.

Nah, not a chance.

Here was Isella, rising to his feet, to declare: "Here's to Yuri. May the Russians release all of the Jews and all of the political prisoners. And," he added, not quite as an afterthought, "I hope they're all horse players."

Here was Marty Bass, attempting to compliment Yuri on his courage, emphatically declaring, "You got ———," but using an American expression that Elena said she would have to explain later to her husband.

Here was Mimi DiPietro, describing for Yuri the joys of living in his new Highlandtown neighborhood: "We got decent, respectable people here. We ain't got no crooks, no pimps, no whores. Everybody works here." And then here was Mimi, leaning in close to Yuri and showing him the nuances of tearing apart and ingesting an East Baltimore steamed crab.

"This part I eat?" inquired Yuri.

"No, not that, the hell with that," explained Mimi.

"Delicious," said Yuri, finally diving into some backfin.

"For you," shouted attorney Arnold Weiner from across the table, "they're from the Black Sea."

Now Yuri looked up at all the food, and his eyes began to well up, for reasons having nothing at all to do with the spicy seafood.

"This is a feast," he said slowly. "This is unbelievable, the finest beer, the finest food. And such fine new friends."

He began to talk of those who had helped him arrive here: his wife, who never gave up, and Sen. Barbara Mikulski and Gov. William Donald Schaefer, who went to Yuri's apartment for two hours when he toured the Soviet Union with the Baltimore Symphony Orchestra. "Yes," said Yuri, "he was very nice to me. Tell me, is he running for president?"

"Schaefer? Why do you ask?"

"I have this sticker," Yuri said. "It says, 'Schaefer for President.' "

"He brought that to Moscow?"

"Uh, no. Uh, I don't remember how I got it. Uh, tell me something," he said, quickly shifting gears. "How come Schaefer never mentioned to me this Mimi DiPietro?"

" 'Cause he's a dummy," said DiPietro, momentarily glancing up from a bowl of crab soup.

"We should have sent Mimi over to Moscow to get Yuri out," said Elena Balovlenkov. "It wouldn't have taken 10 years."

"No," said Richard Sher, "they would have sent him out just to get Mimi out of the country."

"Mimi's translator would have defected," said Al Isella.

Now the talk turned to international politics, to the great issues of human rights and the historic nuclear arms treaty that Reagan and Gorbachev soon would be signing.

"I hope this opens a new page between the two countries," said Yuri.

"How about you, Mimi?" somebody asked. "What do you think about these talks in Washington?"

"I didn't hear about it," said Mimi.

"Reagan and Gorbachev," it was explained. "They're meeting at the White House. What do you think?"

"Reagan's a good guy," declared Mimi, making inroads on a crab fluff. "He'll meet anybody."

Now Yuri began to talk of the mad swirl of events in the past two weeks: How he'd gone sleepless for three nights in his Moscow apartment, wondering if the Russians would really let him go this time; how he'd felt "like a soldier in a last battle" as departure day loomed; how they'd made him wait 15 hours to get through customs in Moscow; how he'd sat on the plane, waiting for it to take off and wondering if the KGB would appear at the last moment and pull him away. "Then," he said, "the engine started, and the plane took off, and my tears began. I began to cry. I became hysterics."

It was quiet around the table now. Yuri Balovlenkov put down a glass of American beer, and wiped his lips, and looked back on his ordeal.

"I believe in God. God helped me. In my difficult moments, I prayed. Sometimes all day, all night. Once, I went to a monastery for three days and walked in the woods and prayed. And God must have listened," he said, looking around the table, "because I am in America, and I am eating crabs with my new friends."

"You're a good guy," Mimi DiPietro said now, resting a hand on Yuri's shoulder. "And you live in my neighborhood, which is the best part."

"Yes," said Yuri. "And this is important day in my life, because I meet Mimi DiPietro."

And if that doesn't sound like peace in our time, then what does?

DECEMBER 10, 1987

RACE

Refusing to Give Up

When the Baltimore Orioles opened their 1992 season at Camden Yards, the Reverend Jesse Jackson showed up to give all the television stations something to cover besides baseball. They could cover him. He wished to make a statement he considered very important and some others considered very silly. He called the front-office integration of baseball one of the most pressing problems facing black America.

What made this declaration fundamentally sad was geography, and time. Just a few blocks from the ballpark is a thoroughfare known as Martin Luther King Boulevard. It had been 24 years since King's assassination when Jackson, King's spiritual heir, showed up and failed completely to take notice of low-rent housing complexes called Lexington Terrace and Poe Homes while decrying the troubles of baseball.

At this time in America, the average major league baseball player makes about $1.2 million. Per year. The last time the city of Baltimore counted—which was 1990—Lexington Terrace and Poe Homes had median household incomes of not quite $5,000. Also per year. And virtually every one of the thousands of people living there is black.

There's pain in any discussion of race relations. It's the sore that never heals, the constant reminder that we never quite live up to all the stuff they teach in civics classes about the American melting pot.

This city came pretty close to destroying itself in 1968, in the calamitous aftermath of the King assassination. When the smoke cleared, anxiety took over. Downtown became ghostly after dark. Thousands of white families with money either fled to suburbia or enrolled their children in private schools. Then thousands of middle-class black families did the same.

What saved us was a lot of people, black and white, refusing to give up—including three mayors, named Schaefer, Burns, and Schmoke, who never played the race card when lesser men might have.

The city of Baltimore is about 60 percent black—a stunning figure when compared with surrounding counties: Carroll (3 percent black), Harford (8 percent), Howard (12 percent), Anne Arundel (12 percent), and Baltimore County (8 percent).

For a long time, those '68 riots, and the sense that we'd danced very close to the final flame, propelled a sense of cooperation in the city. We'd witnessed our own power of destructiveness, and it terrified us.

But, just as time heals wounds, sometimes it also makes us forget. In the closing years of the century, some old, color-blind relations have begun to look a little frazzled.

LIVED TOO EARLY; DIED TOO SOON

This is about Richard Winborne, who arrived too early for his own good and departed too soon for everybody else's. You never read about him in the newspapers or saw his face on television. He was passed over. History consigned his generation of black people to a kind of national attic of the psyche, period pieces to be pulled out of a trunk and studied on some future rainy day.

When he died last week, at 62, he became one more of those who leave with "might-have-been" stamped next to their names.

For a long time, he cut hair in a beat-up little barbershop on Greenmount Avenue, just above North. The barbershop was a kind of refugee center for the rootless, a hangout for everybody considered invisible by the outside world: people whose skin color had given America license to hold them back, who'd created their own underground life style and economy because that's all that was open to them.

When the civil rights movement finally arrived, they were society's leftovers. Into the barbershop came the one-time beauty now strung out on heroin, who wore dresses that seemed to have wilted over her wasted frame and who tried vainly to use sex to support her drug habit.

Then there were the guys who ran numbers, and those who shot craps out in the alley. When the cops came and banged their nightsticks on the cement, the shooters left their money on the ground and waited in the barbershop for a few minutes. The cops picked the money off the ground and drove away. The shooters shrugged their shoulders and said it was part of the game. They called the money ground rent.

There were the street hustlers, and the aimless, and the evangelicals with their boundless belief in a God who seemed a little slow to make his presence known in such shabby places. Richard Winborne was one of the street people, and yet he wasn't.

He made all his money cutting hair, and he preached a little gospel on Sundays, and he worked in the beat-up old barbershop and listened carefully. He knew about politics and psychology, and history and human nature. He was sensitive and insightful, and the gentlest of men.

But he'd arrived too soon, long before any civil rights movement, long before equal opportunities, long before affirmative action programs. America hadn't yet developed a conscience in those days, or a sense of guilt, or a fear that showed its face. Richard Winborne belonged to a generation that grew up not knowing how to raise its voice.

By the time opportunities arrived, he was too tired, too defeated, too filled with responsibilities to start over.

He sat in the barbershop one spring day, not long after the riots of '68, and he looked out on Greenmount Avenue and said: "These young kids are asking themselves, 'Why can't we run our own neighborhoods?' You know, that never occurred to anybody when I was coming up. The Italians run their own neighborhoods. The Jews and the Poles run their own neighborhoods. Why can't we?" He spoke in a high-pitched voice full of delight at the thought. He pointed a finger at stores up and down the block, all owned by white people, with white people working all the jobs inside.

Things started changing after the riots. The government, frightened at the prospect of more trouble, created antipoverty programs. Busy-work jobs were created. Richard Winborne was never impressed.

"It's all based on fear," he said one day, "and you can't run a country on fear. People are engrossed in fear, and it's all unfounded and feeds on itself. White people are just buying time with these programs. They're afraid, because objects were burned. They still don't understand the desperation that provoked it."

He thought the big economic break of his life came in the early '70s, when a job opened as a guard at the city jail. There were five kids at home then, and here was a chance to make more money than he'd ever known.

But it didn't last. The tension, and the constant noise of the place, rattled him badly. His blood pressure soared. He withdrew from the prison business and went back to barbering. A few years back, he had a stroke that left him partly paralyzed, and he lived out the remaining couple of years of his life in a one-room apartment above a laundromat on lower Park Heights Avenue, dragging his arm behind him.

The ones like Richard Winborne never made it into newspaper headlines or television broadcasts. His generation was put aside, to be remembered on a rainy day yet to be announced. This was that rainy day.

FEBRUARY 3, 1987

RETIRING JUDGE ONCE BARELY AVOIDED JAIL

They put Judge Joseph Howard's portrait on a wall in the U.S. court-house here yesterday, far away from the welcome sign they gave him on Harford Avenue in 1958.

It was his first hour in this city. With less luck and less justice, he might have spent his second hour behind bars. He'd driven a battered station wagon here from Des Moines, Iowa, stuffed with everything he owned, and now he was looking for his brother's house at 1017 Bona-parte Street.

Utterly lost and frustrated, circling Harford Avenue for the third or fourth time, Howard finds himself stopped by two white police officers who ordered him out of his car.

"You've been driving this wreck around these streets for three months," one officer charges. "When the hell are you gonna get a Mary-land license?"

Howard boils and says something caustic. The cop takes offense. In a moment, the two are locked in physical struggle, which Howard is winning by virtue of sheer size.

Suddenly, the second cop breaks it up. "Stop it, John," he shouts at his partner. "You're wrong. Just let him go."

And Joe Howard, who might have been on his way to jail, is instead allowed to pursue the rest of his life: as a city prosecutor, as a Supreme Bench judge, and as a federal judge who finally declared, at age 69, that it's time to "slow down," as he became a senior judge—where he'll assume a lightened caseload—and watched them hang his portrait yes-terday in an honored spot at the federal courthouse.

Such are the whims of fate, though, that everything could have turned in that flash of a moment on Harford Avenue 34 years ago—in a moment that, years after it happened, never left Howard's memory. "It would have destroyed my whole career before it started," he said. He was sitting in his old Supreme Bench chambers above St. Paul Street a while back, weighing not only his own life but, implicitly, a history of racial edginess in this country.

"If that one white policeman hadn't been honest, they would have pulled me in," he said. "I would have been taken to District Court. The police would have given a false story. And the judge would have rejected my denial. The judge would have said, 'I'm sure this officer wouldn't lie,' and I would have been found guilty of something. That's the usual procedure."

All through his career, some would have said: "That's Joe Howard, talking with a chip on his shoulder." He's led with his instincts, with his nerve endings exposed. He's heard charges of playing the race card. Invariably, though, he's backed up his instincts with painful facts.

A quarter-century ago, as an assistant state's attorney, Howard charged there was a double standard in rape cases: tough sentences for blacks who raped white women, a shrug of the shoulders for whites who raped black women.

Cries of outrage were heard from judges across the state who heard his words. Prove it, they said. A year later, he did. A 32–page report with 15 statistical charts showed a clear pattern of heavy sentences against black rapists and light ones for white rapists.

When he was appointed to a seat on the old Supreme Bench a few years later, one worried sitting judge whispered that Howard might turn the swearing-in into a black power conference. Howard laughed ruefully when he heard about the remark. But, by 1975, he was hammering at a court system that had historically denied jobs to blacks and women.

Howard's race consciousness comes from a lifetime of feeling like an outsider. His mother was a Sioux, his father an African-American who was friends with Dr. Ralph Bunche, United Nations undersecretary general. Howard remembers accompanying his father and Dr. Bunche as they left the U.N. building and took a New York subway. Charles R. Howard rose to give his seat to a white woman. The woman sat down next to Bunche, took note of his skin color, and immediately got up and walked away. Dr. Bunche looked sadly at his friends. "When I get out of the U.N. and take public transportation," he said, "I'm just another nigger."

And yet, given that history, Howard has sometimes seemed inordinately sensitive to white defendants. He decried police who seemed particularly tough on white political protesters. He worried about sending white defendants into prisons where they'd be racially outnumbered and vulnerable to attack.

Through the years, Joseph Howard became a kind of lightning rod for attacks: some of it based on preconceptions of a black man in a white man's traditional position, some of it based on language aimed at undoing generations of legal unfairness, much of it a microcosm of America's ongoing sensitivity between blacks and whites.

And all of it follows a moment on Harford Avenue 34 years ago, in his first hour in Baltimore, when one white city cop with a sense of fairness helped change a man's fate, and a judicial system's.

FEBRUARY 18, 1992

HIGH-RISE LIVING IN THE OTHER BALTIMORE

There ought to be a dateline on this piece, the way newspapers put datelines on stories from faraway places. This dateline should say: The Other Baltimore. It's so far away, a lot of people pretend it doesn't exist.

This slice of the Other Baltimore is the 200 block of North Fremont Avenue, in West Baltimore. It's where the great renaissance of the city is only a rumor.

You leave Charm City the moment you hit Fremont Avenue. When you climb to the 14th floor of the Lexington Terrace public housing project, you can stand in an outdoor corridor and peer through the wire fence erected to keep people from falling to the ground, and you see handsome buildings not too far away, except that they're on the other side of the world.

"We're not even on the map," says a muscular kid who says his name is TNT. "We're only word of mouth to downtown folks."

"Ask about the rats and the roaches in this building," says a lanky kid named David, standing outside the high-rise, next to TNT. "They always there. I seen a rat, I hit him upside the head with a stick."

In the Lexington Terrace project are 14 floors with seven hundred apartments. In most there are women with children but no men. In virtually all, the residents are black. You walk through apartments and see living rooms with nothing on their cement floors, and the only decorations are photos cut from magazines and then pasted on the walls, and the kitchen shelves have roach spray next to the Frosted Flakes.

"The roach spray don't do nothing," a woman on the 11th floor says bitterly. "It's just something the roaches get high on. It shakes 'em up for 30 or 40 minutes, and then they go on their way."

On the 10th floor, you enter an apartment where the living room screens are ripped out. "It was on this floor," says Bobby Cheeks, shaking his head sadly.

"Just like this screen," says a woman who lives here.

"The baby wasn't no more than a year old," says another woman.

They keep talking about the baby. Bobby Cheeks is walking through the high-rise corridors today as director of the Welfare Rights Organization, which wants all families with children moved out of these high-rises for reasons that include the child on the 10th floor.

There are 18 public high-rises in this city, half of them in West Baltimore. The buildings are crowded, and crime is high. There are so many floors, and so many apartments and corridors, that lawbreakers find it easy to hide here. Some women say they push their refrigerators against their front doors for protection at night. Cheeks wants the city to admit this is no place for children.

"The baby was just one reason," he says.

The baby fell 10 floors. The window screen in the baby's apartment was torn, and the baby leaned onto the windowsill from a chair and then fell out the window.

It was a couple of years ago, and yet people who live here still talk about it because they have children of their own, and because the screens are still torn in many of the apartments, and because they live high off the ground.

The baby's mother wasn't home. The baby went to sleep, and the mother went out to get food stamps, and the baby woke up alone. Miraculously, the child lived after falling 10 floors. The mother came home. They lived in the apartment another three years before moving away.

Bobby Cheeks assumes a kind of fury when he talks about places like this. He grew up on these streets and has carved out a life working with welfare families. A lot of people don't like him. They think the welfare system's gone too far, that families are now locked into a mentality that assumes the world owes them a living.

But who could call this living? The noise is constant. There are grafitti on the walls, and the scrawl adds to the cramped feeling in the corridors. There's trash in the stairwells, and the odor of human waste. The elevators work only when they're in the mood. The apartments are tiny, and there are people in them who haven't any idea how to get out.

Bobby Cheeks says he's walked through hallways in the high-rises and stumbled over junkies with needles still sticking out of their arms, who don't bother to hide what they're doing.

They're a part of this city we don't want to see. They're in the newspaper every day, but there ought to be a dateline on the stories that says: The Other Baltimore.

JUNE 5, 1984

TALKING HONESTLY IS SOMETIMES PAINFUL

On the afternoon of April 9, 1968, in the final gasp of the Baltimore riots, the crowd swelled over every bloody inch of Pennsylvania Avenue and Mosher Street and watched as Melvin D. Williams stood on a wooden platform and shouted words into a microphone. "It's all over," he declared. "Go home."

In that instant, you could hear the world quiet down.

"It's over," he said again. "There will be no more rioting."

Quickly, and quietly, the streets emptied out. I was at the back of the crowd, dazed after four days and nights of fire and rage, and turned to the guy next to me.

"Who was that?" I asked.

"That's Little Melvin," the guy said, looking at me as if I'd just arrived from some distant planet.

"But who is he?"

"Oh," the guy said, weighing his words, "just call him 'a popular figure on The Avenue.' "

By the morning of January 15, 1987, which is the anniversary of Dr. Martin Luther King's birth, Melvin D. Williams had become less popular, but not exactly less visible.

Pickets marched in front of the *Baltimore Sun* newspaper building on that day, and one carried a sign that read, "Little Melvin is the *Sun*'s Birthday Gift to King," and maybe 70 of these pickets chanted "We are not pushers, we are people."

On the front steps of the building, the Reverend Walter S. Thomas, pastor of the New Psalmist Baptist Church, said, "Du Burns is news. Kurt Schmoke and Parren Mitchell are news. Is Little Melvin news?"

For five days, the *Sun* had run a masterful series on Melvin Williams, by reporter David Simon, called "Easy Money: Anatomy of a Drug Empire."

Was it news?

Absolutely.

Not 25 yards from the platform where Melvin Williams spoke on that humid April afternoon in 1968 there was a drug program called Project Adapt. The place was an absolute rat hole—bleak, falling apart, and filled with nearly a thousand addicts who would line up every day for methadone to try to beat their heroin habits.

And they were just a tiny piece of the drug traffic in Baltimore, just a sliver of Melvin Williams's gift to the community.

Inside Project Adapt one day, a caseworker named Pablo Gonzales pointed through a window to Mosher Street, where junkies nodded off on cement steps.

"Look at 'em," he said. "They're out there blind and pickled and falling over each other. And there's more of them every damned day."

Now the city talks of twenty thousand heroin addicts, and of far more cocaine addicts, and of kids breaking into houses to support their habits, and of knocking down old ladies on the street, and all of them and the people who feed their habits are the children of Melvin D. Williams.

Is Little Melvin news?

Yes, even from his prison cell.

On the front page of this newspaper last week, as pickets behind him decried the articles on Williams, Baltimore City councilman Nathaniel McFadden said, "I question the timing. Why now? Why did it have to run when we're marking Dr. King's birthday? I just want this newspaper to be more sensitive to our community."

Was it insensitive to tell Melvin Williams's story on Martin Luther King's birthday?

Of course.

At this newspaper, we're insensitive all the time, to blacks and to other human beings, too. We're not proud of it. We'd like to be nicer people. But we put out a newspaper 365 days a year, and in the process of interpreting the world on short notice every day, we sometimes forget to look ahead more than a day at a time.

Does this make insensitivity excusable?

Nope.

But nobody in this office said, "Hey, let's run the Melvin series during the Martin Luther King observances," any more than anybody said, "Let's run a Jeffrey Levitt savings and loan exposé during Hanukkah" a year ago.

Both just worked out that way. The news doesn't particularly break on schedule. On Calvert Street, Councilman McFadden was perfectly reasonable when he asked if any black editors had a hand in the series.

Nope. There are no black editors on the metro desk here. There have been black editors here, but one by one they have moved elsewhere and, for several weeks now, there have been none. Others will be hired. It is part of the ongoing process of bringing black people into the American mainstream, to try to help interpret black America to whites who still don't understand.

Ironically, blacks used to complain that the daily papers didn't cover the black community. And they were right. On a newspaper where I once worked, police radios sat on the city desk and sputtered out breaking crime reports. If you listened carefully, you sometimes heard an echo.

"Got a shooting," a reporter monitoring the broadcasts would say.

"Where is it?" an editor would ask.

"West Baltimore," the reporter would say.

"Ah, just another bunch of blacks," the editor would say. The stories never made the paper. An entire community was being written out of the human race. In the newsroom, you swallowed your revulsion.

On Calvert Street now, the pickets were asking, Why does the *Sun* run so many negative stories on the black community?

That question hurts. On the issues involving race, this has always been a liberal voice in an often hostile environment. Our problem is: How do you say conditions are bad without saying negative things? You write about drugs, because this is what generations of poverty and anger and despair have bred. Is it negative to say that?

I thought it was our way of issuing a cry on behalf of the otherwise voiceless: "Attention! Attention must be paid! Things have been bad for too long!"

Melvin Williams wasn't just a dope dealer tearing at the veins of a community. To too many people, he once really was a popular figure on The Avenue. Now, black people have learned not to talk about him in such terms. White-run newspapers are just beginning to talk about him at all.

The two of us—blacks and whites—are still learning how to talk honestly to each other. And sometimes the process involves pain.

JANUARY 18, 1987

STAYING TO WORK IT OUT

In a little corner of St. Elizabeth's Roman Catholic Church in East Baltimore, James Radowski holds up one brown hiking shoe. He says someone threw it at his head.

"Those schoolkids," he says.

"Tell him about the folding chair they threw," says a woman one seat away.

"Tell him about the textbooks," says someone else.

Voices are muted in their anger, because this is a church. But the voices will be rising through this entire evening as the church fills nearly to capacity. East Baltimore has been mobilized, first by the baseball-bat clubbing of a kid named Expedito "Pedro" Lugo, then by the outpouring of voices declaring a general condition of unsafe streets every time the students from Hampstead Hill Middle School make their way through the neighborhood.

"The textbooks," a woman says, pulling a few of them out of a brown shopping bag.

And now, eyes blazing with outrage, James Radowski holds up one big book and then another. "They threw this at us," he says. The book is *Life Science* and it weighs several pounds. "They threw this at us," he says again. This book is *World History*, and it weighs several pounds more.

Radowski lives on South Robinson Street directly across from Hampstead Hill, where the book-throwers attend school. Standing on his block one afternoon last week, you could hear a voice inside a third-floor classroom bellowing at students for minutes at a time, and when a bell rang to change classes, there were sounds like flak bursting inside the building.

"There's the problem," city councilman Carl Stokes was saying later.

"It's not just a problem in the neighborhood. It's a problem for all the kids in the school who are trying to get an education."

Stokes was standing in front of the big crowd inside St. Elizabeth's. He was black, and most of the crowd was white.

A sense of perspective must be kept here. Yes, most of the kids from Hampstead Hill are black. Yes, the neighbors are mostly white. But, no, it doesn't mean that all of these black kids are running rampant. And, no, it doesn't mean that whites who are complaining are merely verbalizing hidden racist inclinations. A neighborhood has been under siege here, and painting easy racial stereotypes helps nothing.

The issue is those kids who have terrorized a neighborhood for years while people in power were looking the other way, and the issue is what, having finally acknowledged the problem, the city of Baltimore will do to make it better, while there's still time.

"Let me tell you something," says William Bohler. He's 86 years old and peers across a church pew through thick eyeglasses. "I've lived here all my life, and I didn't see in the riots of 1968 what I see some mornings now, the hollering and the looting. But it's not racial, and I'll tell you why. It's black and white kids. Fairmont and Lakewood, kids banging on everything. Luzerne Avenue, the kids running wild. And then these juvenile courts that don't enforce the law. They just release the kids to the parents, who are the ones to blame for not teaching the kids right from wrong in the first place."

It's instructive to hear a voice like Bohler's. Resist the temptation to cry race, he's saying. It gets us nowhere. Resist the temptation to call every kid a troublemaker. It just isn't true.

Also, though: resist the temptation to call white East Baltimoreans racist because they're asking the removal of troublesome black kids from their neighborhood. It's too easy, and it isn't fair.

These are the white people who didn't desert the city at the first sighting of black faces in their neighborhoods. They're not the ones who found God in suburbia in the great white migration of the last three decades.

They stayed. They aren't the living room liberals who sneaked out of town, who always gave lip service to the philosophy of integration until it actually arrived in their own neighborhoods, whereupon they fled.

These are the ones who didn't talk a good game, they just stayed and lived their lives and tried to cope with tensions passed down to them from a succession of previous generations.

"Can we make it work?" Ed Rutkowski asks. He thinks about the question for a moment. Rutkowski is president of the Baltimore-Linwood Neighborhood Association. He's an engineer by profession, a man who grew up in Highlandtown and chaired last week's meeting at St. Elizabeth's.

"Yeah," he says, "we can make it work. The schools will be integrated, and the neighborhoods will be integrated, and that's OK. Integration is workable. It's already here. People here won't move because of integration. Those who do, we can live without. It isn't the color of people, it's the kind of people. It's absentee landlords who don't care what kind of people they rent to. It doesn't take very many tenants who aren't good, who don't take care of the property, before people start moving."

In East Baltimore, you can feel it quicker than in many neighborhoods. On little streets of row houses packed tightly together, intimacy is automatic. There's a ripple effect every time something goes wrong.

In America, we tend to translate lots of problems into racial differences. East Baltimore can do it differently. There's an edginess in the air, but there's also a sense of working things out without hostility.

If they can do this, it'll be a lesson to the rest of this race-obsessed nation.

JUNE 2, 1991

SPORTS

"I Sit in These Bleachers, and Close My Eyes, and It's All Still Going On"

Sports offer us grand illusion. We enter the ballpark for a few hours, and it almost seems like childhood. It's Ripken going into the hole, but it's a vision of our formerly youthful selves turning the base hit into a double play. It was Unitas throwing to Berry and Moore across all those autumns, but it was our wanna-be selves hearing the crowd calling our own name.

Around here, for the longest time, the grandest illusion about sports was that it was something besides a business. It's been a terrible learning process: the loss of the Colts, who were a religion; the loss of the basketball Bullets, who couldn't draw enough people because downtown was too scary when they played here; and the threatened removal of the Orioles to Washington, before cooler heads prevailed.

Through it all, though, some wonderful personalities have transcended the business deals and the extortion efforts and the bullying owners. They're the ones who make it worthwhile; they lift us out of the incessant news of fresh street crimes, of numbing routine at the office. Also, they form our common community denominator.

BROOKS ROBINSON ENTERS THE HALL OF FAME

COOPERSTOWN, N.Y.—He looked across the pasture and saw a sea of orange. And the sea cried out, "Brooks . . . Brooks . . . Brooks." And the sound swept across the pasture, and it raised the flesh on your arms, and it was good.

Brooks Robinson must have felt he'd never left home.

They inducted the Baltimore Oriole, the man who ad-libbed around third base for 23 summers, into the Hall of Fame yesterday, in a pasture awash with Baltimore people with orange Brooks Robinson shirts on their backs and a collective lump in their throats.

It was the outpouring of a kind of extended family. Mayor Schaefer and Baltimore County Executive Don Hutchinson stood at one side of the crowd, and Wild Bill Hagy at the other, contorting their bodies like pretzels and leading hometown cheers that rang like love calls.

These people had watched Robinson for two decades in the grass in Baltimore, and now they had come by car and by bus and by van to this tiny village in upstate New York to thank him for the memories.

Robinson did not forget them.

"And then I count another blessing," he said. "That is Baltimore. That is Baltimore. And playing in that city, I share this day with my adopted hometown, which supported Brooks Robinson on good and bad days . . . Baltimore, thank you, I love you all."

And the thousands of Baltimoreans who filled the pasture in front of him, who have overwhelmed this village of some 2,500 inhabitants as it has never been filled before, roared their love back at him.

Since Friday, the streets here have been clogged with people in Oriole shirts and caps, and hotel rooms reportedly have been booked for miles around. In Oneonta, 22 miles away, Town House Motor Inn owner Bill Boggs said, "We had some Baltimore police come through here Saturday night with sleeping bags. There were gonna sleep in a field. A father and son slept on my parking lot in their car.

"Last winter, when it was announced that Brooks Robinson was voted in, within two hours there was a thousand-room shortage. My phones never stopped. I've lived here all my life. Believe me, the closest thing to this was Mickey Mantle's induction, and there weren't half as many people for that."

If baseball captures so much of what we like to believe about ourselves—our sense of youth, our playfulness, our good nature—then Robinson is the game's personification, the crew-cut youngster who grew into graceful adulthood, the model of ascending temperament, the mortal man blessed with immortal reflexes.

Yesterday, he kept coming back to his blessings.

"I must be the luckiest man in the world," he said. "I keep asking, how could any one man be so fortunate? It's more than any one human being could ask for."

He thanked his managers and teammates, and his family, and he thanked his wife, Connie, and then, almost in a whisper, said, "Thank you for everything, darling."

And the sea of orange roared its thanks again.

"The thing about Brooks," said Don Hutchinson, "is that he still doesn't understand the amount of affection people have for him. He's the same guy now that he always was. Not a piece of this has gone to his head."

And yet he joined the immortals of the game yesterday. Some of them sat behind him—DiMaggio, Koufax, Warren Spahn, Cool Papa Bell, Bill Terry, Duke Snider, the Baltimore kid Al Kaline.

Robinson walked onto the induction stand looking shy and a little self-conscious, as though maybe a mistake had been made, that he'd gotten in on a pass somehow but was thrilled about it anyway.

But there was no mistake.

The Chicago announcer Jack Brickhouse, inducted into the broadcasters' wing here yesterday, told the crowd, "Immediately on arriving here, I saw a blur. That had to be Brooks Robinson, going to his left."

Baseball Commissioner Bowie Kuhn said, "I never saw a man dominate a single event like Brooks Robinson in the 1970 World Series."

In the sea of orange in the pasture, they knew differently. They saw him in his youth, and there never was anyone like him. He not only made the utterly impossible plays afield and stroked the base hits when ballgames were on the line, but he immersed himself in the fabric of the community.

"This is a day for my giving thanks," Robinson said, "and this is the life from which I want to give back."

And yet he's always done that.

The ballplayers live our fantasy lives. They play the games for us by proxy, and we tell ourselves that their lives are as exemplary off the field as on, and we want to believe it.

We want the myths to take hold. The stories are too good to let go. Babe Ruth points to his home run landing spot, and heals sick children in his spare time. The legends take on lives of their own.

With Brooks Robinson, they exist only in the truth. The sea of orange called out his name yesterday, the way they always did at Memorial Stadium. But they cheered as much for the man as the ballplayer.

This town celebrates the magnificence of athletes, but also the glory of youth.

You walk into the Hall of Fame, and a sign tells you that Abner Doubleday stood here 119 years ago, in farmer Phinney's pasture, and invented the game of baseball. The sign calls Doubleday "the lad in the pasture." But the sign is wrong.

Brooks Robinson looked across the sea of orange yesterday and must have felt he'd never left home, and for everyone, he was the lad in the pasture.

AUGUST 31, 1983

LOYALTY IS NOTHING

"What'll we do with ourselves this afternoon?" cried Daisy, "and the day after that, and the next 30 years?"

"Don't be morbid," Jordan said. "Life starts all over again when it gets crisp in the fall."

—F. Scott Fitzgerald, *The Great Gatsby*

Not any more, it doesn't.

There are to be no more late autumn afternoons at Memorial Stadium. Game called on account of greed. Robert Irsay is taking his football team to Indianapolis.

Do we listen to our heads or our hearts? Our heads say: The community is better off without Irsay. Indianapolis can have him. Getting this man in your town is like getting food poisoning. But our hearts say: Something precious and irreplaceable has died, not just a football team but a love affair between a team and a town that transcended athletics and even, once, transcended money.

When the moving vans appeared in the dark of night at the Colts complex, it was a message to every city in America that has a team owned by somebody from out of town: Nothing is forever. Loyalty means nothing. Money is all.

And so, before the body is entirely cold, the mind does backflips through a 31-year history.

Once there was Unitas throwing heart-stopping passes to Raymond Berry in the overtime dusk at Yankee Stadium. Once there was Matte and the wrist band on the frozen turf at Green Bay. Once there were Marchetti and Donovan and Parker and Moore, people whose names symbolized not only a football team but a way of life in this town.

Once there was a kid named Joe Ehrmann. In the twilight at Memorial Stadium, in sudden-death overtime, a little guy named Toni Linhart had kicked the Colts into the 1975 championship play-offs.

Moments later, in the steamy Colts locker room there was Ehrmann, blubbering, "Those people out there, they're unbelievable. I'd like to hug 'em all, one by one, honest to goodness I would."

Now there is no hugging, except by mourners at the grave site. Memorial Stadium on autumn days becomes a kind of sacred burial ground for memories of the Baltimore Colts.

Is Robert Irsay aware of any of this? He can take his team to the brand new Hoosier Dome in Indianapolis, and for a few moments he'll feel the new town's warmth, and for a while he'll feel as though he's beginning his life again.

But something dies in the process, called trust. In the towns of America, people are watching. Sports depends on the emotional ties of communities to teams, or it doesn't work.

Without trust, there are no ties. Ballgames become mere diversions, to be attended when there's nothing better to do and the weather is suitable. The communities hold back their devotion, knowing it's only their team on loan.

When you present mere diversions, you don't have people filling every seat in a stadium every year, one autumn following another, the way the Colts did for so long.

A marriage doesn't exist when one partner offers love and the other says, "Talk to my lawyer about it."

This was a 31-year marriage that began to end a dozen years ago, maybe more. Something died when the team was shifted from the old

National Football League to the American Football Conference.

It was still the same Colts on the field, but who were those strange guys they were playing now, and where was Vince Lombardi and where was old George Halas prowling the enemy sidelines at Memorial Stadium the way they had for so many years?

These were strangers now who'd suddenly come into our home ballpark.

The marriage got worse. The original husband, Carroll Rosenbloom, traded away his wife for the Los Angeles Rams. The new husband, Robert Irsay, moved in with some pretty terrible habits. He was abusive. He drank and made threats and never got anybody's name right in his own new family.

And then the old man started sleeping around, and one of his ladies of the night fell for his sweet talk and his football team.

Now he's followed through on his threat to leave, and we watch him exit with a sense of bitter relief, except for this: The bum took the children, too.

Once upon a time, the Baltimore Colts were an earth force in this town. They played football in the sunlight before throngs of people living at the top of their lungs.

Now, Irsay sends moving vans on a snowy night, and no one is there to say goodbye.

Barry Levinson made a movie called *Diner,* in which a fellow refuses to marry his girl until she passes a quiz on the Baltimore Colts. In places around America, audiences laughed at the crazy thought.

People in Baltimore didn't laugh. It seemed perfectly reasonable. Who could marry somebody who didn't know John Unitas's jersey number?

Once, we were innocents. Pro football raised itself to a point of such religious self-promotion that the aroma of incense blotted out the stench of greed.

Now we know better.

What will we do tomorrow, and the day after that, and the next 30 years? The good news: On Sunday afternoons in late autumn, we'll have lots of time now to do the things we always wanted to do.

The bad news: What we always wanted to do was watch the Baltimore Colts.

MARCH 30, 1984

THE TAMING OF WILD BILL HAGY

In the bottom of the first inning, three Baltimore batters struck out. This was not considered such a wonderful sign. It meant that the Orioles, only one inning into the 1988 season, were already in midseason form, vintage 1987.

In Section 34 of the upper deck, where pandemonium once reigned, a cab driver from Dundalk named William Hagy slugged on a container of beer and shook his woolly head ruefully. He is a shy, retiring sort, as everyone knows, but once, when he was called Wild Bill and contorted his Play-Doh body into shapes roughly resembling the letters o-r-i-o-l-e-s, he sent out waves of adrenalin that electrified a stadium.

"My life as a public figure is done," Hagy was saying yesterday in Section 34, even before the Orioles had gone down to cheerless, ignominious defeat, 12–0, to the Milwaukee Brewers.

He sat in relative obscurity. Gone was his big cowboy hat, replaced by a modest beer cap. Gone were any inclinations to strut atop the Orioles dugout, to orchestrate an entire ballpark into organized frenzy. Gone, too, were the chants that originated in 34 and used to rumble through the park:

"Come on, Ken, put it in the bullpen."

"Come on, Lowenstein, put it over the beer sign."

More than anyone else in this town, Wild Bill Hagy is the man who liberated the souls of Baltimore baseball fans, who unchained the municipal id. Once upon a time, even in the most wildly successful Orioles seasons, fans here were among the most uptight in all of baseball, self-conscious, meek, impossible to coax into unbuttoned enthusiasm.

Hagy's the one who made it cool to come to the ballpark and open your mouth. From Section 34, Insanity Central, the enthusiasm and the energy and the people living at the edge of their composure spread outward.

"Wild Bill and his gang changed everything," Elrod Hendricks was saying on the field before yesterday's game. Hendricks, whose career as player and coach here spans two decades, remembers the pre-Hagy days, when fans sat on their hands.

"He got the fans to join the Orioles," Hendricks said. "Him and his wild bunch, the rowdies. It caught on, in the whole ballpark. It even caught on in the dugout. We'd be down, and I can remember Dempsey,

Singleton, Bumbry, they'd wave towels up at the gang in 34, hoping they'd stir things up."

"Man, I remember when I played, it sometimes seemed like we were an afterthought," Brooks Robinson was saying in the dugout before yesterday's game. Robinson, the unparalleled third baseman, still remembers World Series and play-off games here in front of empty seats.

"Today," he said, "guys around the country tell me they've never seen anything like Baltimore. You go around town, you listen to the talk shows, everybody talks about opening day, opening day. People tell me it's not like this anywhere else in baseball.

"And I remember when it wasn't like that here. It used to be all Colts when I played. You went to a Colts game, it was a happening. But now, it's like that with the Orioles, and I think Wild Bill had a lot to do with that."

Is it only coincidence that Wild Bill ceased his public gyrations midway into the 1984 season, after the Orioles' World Series championship of the previous fall, and the club's on-field performance has turned dreadful ever since?

Once, in the early '80s, there was a phrase known as Orioles Magic. At Memorial Stadium one night when Wild Bill still reigned supreme, it began to rain. In Section 34, the faithful took up a chant:

"Wild Bill, make it stop. Wild Bill, make it stop."

And then a wonderful thing happened. Hagy got to his feet, and he took off his big cowboy hat, and he began sweeping it in great circles above his head, as though soaking up moisture. In moments, the rain stopped. In those giddy days, it was considered just a routine miracle.

"Not really a lot to cheer about any more," Hagy was saying yesterday. "But that's not why I stopped coming out. Part of it, it was the beer thing. I used to fill my cooler for $4.50 and buy a $3 ticket. Then they said you couldn't bring a cooler in, and it winds up costing me $20 for a game. That was the final straw.

"The other thing, though, it was wearing itself out. It started becoming something I had to do instead of something I wanted to do. We had a good run for about seven years. I think we taught people to have fun at the park."

Now, when fans yell, "Wild Bill, make it stop," they're probably talking about the Orioles' troubles on the playing field.

APRIL 5, 1988

O'S FOR 21

On the Baltimore *Sun* newspaper, there's a reporter named John Schid-lovsky. The paper's bureau chief in Beijing, he is occasionally given to wearing his Orioles baseball cap on the streets of that ancient Chinese city.

Beijing has been assaulted by spring sandstorms for the last week, but one day a motorist spotted Schidlovsky and bravely rolled down his window and shouted across the street.

"Oh-and-14," he cried, and then drove on. Schidlovsky knew exactly what he meant. Beijing is 12 thousand miles from Baltimore, but Schid-lovsky says he's been getting almost daily multilingual ribbing about the winless, wingless Orioles, whose 1988 record has extended itself to 0-and-21 as this is written.

In the city of Baltimore, which once cheered the now-departed John Unitas Colts and the now-departed Earl Monroe Bullets and the wishes-he-was-departed Frank Robinson Orioles, we are now plunging into something that goes beyond any kind of mere municipal despair.

A radio disc jockey named Bob Rivers, angling for some easy public-ity, vows to stay on the air until the Orioles win their first game. He figured, how long can this go on? This was on Tuesday, April 19. And we now have doctors checking Rivers's blood pressure every hour, and florists sending him bouquets, and "Free Bob Rivers" T-shirts being worn around the city.

Motorists travel the streets with their lights on during daylight hours, in a show of support that looks eerily funereal. A psychic healer in Glen Burnie blames the whole losing streak on a kind of collective team guilt. A local bookmaker, checking the odds, declares that some-one betting $100 for the Orioles to lose on Opening Day and then parlaying his winnings with each successive loss would have been up $13 million by the middle of last week.

In Emmitsburg, 20 nuns at Villa Saint Michael said special prayers. Sister Mary Kevin Gallahan sent the Orioles a letter, saying the nuns have seen many "new beginnings" in their years of service.

What they haven't seen—in fact, what no one has ever seen in the 120 years mankind has been keeping records of such things—is the likes of this year's Orioles. Twenty-one straight losses! And not a victory yet!

On opening day, they lost to the Milwaukee Brewers, 12 to 0. When the losing streak went to six games, they fired the manager, Cal Ripken, and hired former slugger Frank Robinson to take over. The losing went on. When they lost their 15th straight, again to Milwaukee, Brewers' broadcaster Bob Uecker quipped, "When they finally win, they'll get a phone call from the president. Only it'll be the president of some other country."

A few days later, still winless, Robinson got a call from Ronald Reagan, extending good wishes. The Orioles promptly went out and lost again. They gave up nine first-inning runs to Kansas City without getting a batter out.

Robinson, fiery in his playing days, has generally kept his cool through all of this. After he'd lost his sixth straight—the exact number at which Ripken had been fired—he walked through the club's front offices and told a secretary, "They just fired me and hired a new manager, a guy from Japan. His name is Win One Soon."

It's nice he's kept his sense of humor. For a lot of people, this losing streak is beyond humor, beyond logic, beyond reality. It's some great cosmic joke, some *Twilight Zone* episode that keeps on going, some curse by a vengeful god playing fast and loose with a few wayward thunderbolts.

To say this city isn't accustomed to such losing is vast understatement. What the hell, no city is. But these are the Orioles, who had baseball's finest win-loss record over 25 years. These were the Orioles of Frank and Brooks Robinson, of Jim Palmer and Boog Powell and Earl Weaver.

Weaver used to flirt with cardiac arrest any time the team wasn't winning. If they were leading 10 to 0, he'd be in the dugout, screaming at players, "We need more runs. Can't anybody hit the damned baseball?"

Last week, Ken Singleton sat in a suburban nightspot called Wurlitzer's, nursing a beer and remembering his time playing the outfield here. Earl Weaver, for all his barely contained hysteria, was supposed to be a genius. How, Singleton was asked, would Earl handle this Orioles team?

"Oh," Singleton said without a hint of a smile, "Earl would be dead by now."

This losing streak might have killed a lot of people. It might have alienated an entire community. But it's bigger than that; it's a life force beyond explanation.

Are we depressed? Nah, it's beyond depression. It's more like awe. Something like this comes along only once in a lifetime (everybody hopes), and all you can do is sit back and admire the damned thing.

APRIL 29, 1988

FORMER COLTS, BIG EXPERTS, ESCHEW THE FAT

Are they beautiful, or what?

Here is Jim Parker, immortal pro football Hall of Famer with a team called the Baltimore Colts, no. 77 in your program and no. 275 on the scales during his svelte playing days.

He's standing in his package goods store at Liberty Heights Avenue and Garrison Boulevard yesterday morning with a tray of ham and eggs and grits in front of him, which, now that you mention it, he seems to be inhaling.

And here is Art Donovan, immortal pro football Hall of Famer with those same Baltimore Colts, no. 70 in your program and no. 270 on the weight chart in his lean (you should pardon the expression) and hungry playing days.

He's a mere shadow of his former self, at 286 pounds a mere slip of a man who has lost 49 pounds since he peaked at 330 and his doctor declared: "Cut out the beer."

"Beer?" said Donovan, seeing much of his reason for living float away.

"And the salami and bologna."

"Salami and bologna?" said Donovan, seeing what was left of his reason for living disappearing. "Doc, why not just cut off my arm?"

At the end of the second week of the new year, I have come to these two men seeking wisdom. I wish to ask them about weight loss, since everyone in North America resolved on New Year's Eve to lose weight and, among us all, we have lost perhaps four ounces.

About weight loss, nobody knows more than Donovan or Parker, who surely lost more weight (and, to be honest, usually put it back on) in more creative ways than any two people on the planet back when they had to weigh in during their playing days.

"I always had a clause in my contract," Donovan was saying yesterday, "that I had to play at 270. So on Fridays, three o'clock in the morning, Don Joyce would pick me up and we'd go to this steam room at Calvert and Saratoga and sit in it till 10:30 in the morning.

"Then we'd shower and dress and go to the weigh-in. I'd step on the scale, it would say 275. I'd take off my sweat shirt and drop 2 pounds. My pants would be another pound and a half. I'd get down to 270 and a half by dropping my underwear. Still too much. So I'd take out my false teeth. Hey, I got onto that scale just the way I came into the world, no clothes, no teeth, no nothing."

After Friday morning weigh-ins, players could eat whatever they wanted—as long as they got their weight back down by the following Friday.

Most would be voracious by then. Donovan remembers Joyce, the ferocious defensive end, "would have five pounds of raw beef stashed in his locker." Gene "Big Daddy" Lipscomb once had a whole turkey and sweet potato pie waiting in front of his locker when he got off the scale.

"You're gonna eat yourself right out of the league," Coach Weeb Ewbank hollered at him. Jim Parker remembers Lipscomb grabbing the turkey by the leg and swinging the whole thing at Ewbank.

"He was hungry," Parker explained.

Donovan would wait a little longer to indulge. His passion was kosher salami and bologna, "but you couldn't eat meat on Friday if you were Catholic. So I'd buy a few pounds of Hebrew National deli, and I'd make sandwiches, and I'd sit in front of the TV set until midnight. And at the stroke of midnight, you never saw anybody tear into a plate of sandwiches like I did."

Donovan and Parker shared at least one method for weight loss: rubber suits. Donovan would get into one and hop into a whirlpool bath. Parker was even more radical.

On hot summer days when the Colts were still training in Westminster, he'd put on a rubber suit, get into his car and turn the heat all the way up, and drive around for an hour.

"I'd lose 8 or 10 pounds an hour," he says now, between mouthfuls of breakfast in his package goods store.

"That wouldn't work any more," somebody familiar with Parker's habits calls across the store. "When he locks himself in the car now, he locks food in with him."

Not to mention, he's lucky he never killed himself with such drastic methods. "There wasn't any emphasis on health back then," Parker remembers. "Every week, you just got the weight off any way you could."

Donovan remembers fasting each week from Tuesday until Friday's weigh-in, with occasional defections for beer. Parker's son David, a kinesiology graduate of the University of Maryland, has recently taken control of his father's diet.

Parker weighs 315—but he's down from about 335.

"Notice," he says, putting aside the remains of his breakfast, "that I didn't eat any of the ham."

For Parker, the key to weight loss is no more red meat, and pure fruit juices instead of any liquor. For Donovan, it's no more beer.

Well, almost no beer.

"I sneak one once in a while," said Donovan. "But don't put that in the paper, or my wife will holler at me."

Maybe that's what the world needs: Art Donovan's wife to holler at us, and Jim Parker's kid to tell us what to eat.

It beats running around in a rubber suit.

JANUARY 10, 1991

TOUCHING KIDS' LIVES

He still looks like his old photographs: the fringe of white hair around the ears, the lean body, the eyes twinkling like a fellow with a secret. In the old photos, he was always surrounded by his kids. They'd gather around him on the track at the back of the school, and then, in that raspy voice of his, Jerry Nathanson would declare: "Gentlemen, we don't finish second."

Of course, they never did. From somewhere in the mid-'50s to somewhere in the late '60s, his track and cross-country teams virtually never lost, and they can keep records forever and they'll never equal the dominance of Nathanson's teams.

But winning and not losing was the least of his contributions.

Back then, he'd say, "The hell with race and religion. You're either a man or you're not."

That's easy to say now, but several decades back, it was considered a breakthrough. Now it's 15 years since he retired, and it still seems blasphemous for City College kids to be running around a track on a spring day without Nathanson barking at them.

"Oh, I miss it," he says, "but I have memories."

They arrive with names: John Bethea and Lud Hayden and Lou Craig, flowing graceful as water over hurdles; and Steve Lamb and Nick Lee, the gold dust quarter-milers; and the great distance runners like Kenny Mason and Mike George and Alvin Rawlings and Joel Kruh.

He remembers Junius Wilson, who chewed on raw onions before meets so he could look back over his shoulder and "breathe his man to death."

And Tony Virgilio, the sprinter who dived at the finish line to win the 100-yard dash and came up bloody and shredded from that cinder track. Virgilio was carried off, all but dead, but came back 20 minutes later and won the 220-yard dash.

And he remembers a kid named Alvin Jenkins, the first black ever to run at City.

"Alvin had to work after school," Nathanson said, "so he couldn't work out with the team. But he'd work out on his own, and he was sheer class. Man, I'll never forget it. It's the final of the championships over at Kirk Field. It's 10 minutes till the mile run. And Jenkins hasn't shown.

"All of a sudden, here he comes up Kirk Avenue. He left work over on Belair Road, and he ran all the way to Kirk Field. He lines right up at the starting line then, and kills everybody in sight to win the mile."

In those days, the most intense meets were when City met ancient rival Poly. And the meet that always comes to Nathanson's mind is 1959 at Clifton Park, when hundreds of people jammed the track infield to watch a close battle.

"It's the mile relay," Nathanson remembered, "and when the race starts, I'm standing just behind the first turn. Here comes Poly's man, and I'm looking for Dick Svehla, our lead man. He's nowhere in sight. Somebody had knocked the baton out of his hand and he's got to go searching through the crowd in the infield to find it. By the time he gets it, we're two hundred yards behind Poly, and there ain't a way in the world we can win it.

"Well, we pick up a little ground on the next two legs. Jimmy Ware runs so hard he passes out as he finishes. Mike Shannon picks up some distance, but when our anchorman, Jack Wagner, gets the baton, we're still way out of it.

"So it's the last stretch now, and here comes Wagner. He's coming from out of nowhere, he's dying, and with five feet to go he dives across the finish line and beats them by inches.

"I tell you, there were books flying, people screaming, and they stopped a baseball game to find out what happened. Wagner is collapsed at the finish line from exhaustion, and this crowd picks up his dead body and carries it all over Clifton Park."

Sometimes Nathanson had to look beyond the stopwatches and the tape measures to put his teams together. He had a boy come out for cross-country in 1961. His name was Marshall Caplan, and he brought Nathanson the thrill of a lifetime without ever winning a race.

"He'd had polio when he was younger," Nathanson remembered, "and it was noticeable in his legs. He worked so hard, though, that I kept him on the team as a reserve and figured I'd let him run in the city's novice race.

"There's two hundred other kids running. I went up to Marshall before the race—now, it's a rough, two and a half miles over Clifton Park's hills—and I told him, 'Look, kid, I just want you to do one thing for me. Just beat one man for me. Don't finish last.'

"Well, we clobbered everybody that day, but the City kids aren't even watching the top finishers. Everybody's watching to see if Marshall can finish the course. I'll never forget it. He came in ahead of 50 guys, people are screaming their lungs out, and he crossed that finish line and sat down on the ground and cried his eyes out."

It was long ago. He says he drops by City once in a while. He doesn't make any grand entrances, doesn't announce ahead of time that he's coming back. He'll just sit in the stands out by the track, and watch, and remember.

"I see all kinds of pictures out here," he said. "Kids I had to pat on the back or kick in the behind. I can still see them running, you know. I sit in those bleachers, and close my eyes, and it's all still going on."

MAY 16, 1985

CRIME

"Just Act Like You Belong"

In our bleakest moments, a kind of siege mentality consumes the city dweller. Even if crime never directly touches us, we read the newspaper headlines every day and feel as if we're rolling the dice with our lives. That crackle in the night: Was it gunfire, or only a truck backfiring? That eerie time between twilight and dark: Can I make it safely from my car to my house? That kid on the corner: Is he watching me, or just hanging out the way kids have always hung out?

We're not sure any more just how bad things are, just how much the fear of crime has gotten even greater than the very acts of crime. But we do know that we're rattled.

I try to look at the human beings behind the headlines: the pregnant widow of the cop shot in the street, the distraught family of the kid who murdered a schoolteacher, the bookmaker treated like a menace to society because nobody's explained the modern rules of criminal perspective to the vice squad cops: Certain acts no longer should concern them, not in a community drowning in serious crime and in lives coming undone.

Take an ordinary morning in Central District Court. Judge Alan Resnick's on the bench, and this woman is brought before him, 28 years old, dark eyed, hollow cheeked. She's partly paralyzed from a stroke and under medication for epilepsy. The charges: possession of narcotics and solicitation for prostitution.

She has her little girl with her, a beautiful child, maybe three years old, wearing a sunsuit and holding tightly to her mother's hand.

"Your honor," says public defender Burt Mazaroff, "the little girl is here not for purposes of sympathy. There was no one to leave her with. The girl is mentally retarded."

Resnick starts to explain legal options to the woman. The little girl starts making high-pitched noises. The woman's trying to listen to the judge and keep the girl calm at the same time.

Now the woman speaks to Resnick in a voice not much above a whisper. She's been to court before, she says, on various charges: drugs, larceny, prostitution, lewdness.

"On these charges," asks Resnick, "did you go to jail, did you get a fine, or what?"

"Yes, sir," she says.

"Yes, sir, what?" says Resnick.

"I don't recall."

The girl is making noises. She's hitting her hand on legal papers and kicking her legs. The woman's eyes are brimming with tears as she tries to calm the child and listen to the voices around her.

"This woman is obviously ill blessed," says public defender Mazaroff.

The little girl's legs are up on the table now. The mother is pleading with her. Mazaroff is waving keys to distract the little girl. Resnick is looking down and trying to keep a sense of order. He has another two dozen cases waiting to be tried.

"I'm agonizing over this," he says.

"Please," the woman whispers to her child.

"Ill blessed," Mazaroff says again, quite softly.

And this is how criminal life is brought to order each day in the city of Baltimore.

LIFE SETTLES DOWN

The morning after the television cameras left, people were standing in the shattered glass at Lombard and Carey Streets in West Baltimore, and everybody pointed fingers.

"Up there," somebody would say.

"Yes."

"My, my."

After a few minutes they'd walk on and another group would come over, trying to relive things, trying to come to grips with the neighborhood kid at the window with the weapons, as they did all day and into the evening on Saturday, the day after Good Friday, the day after six Baltimore policemen were shot in the street on television.

The kid with the guns is named John Earl Williams, a pale, gaunt, blond teenager who managed to sneak an arsenal into his bedroom and unleash it for reasons not yet understood.

The cop who got it the worst was named Jimmy Halcomb. He was a couple of weeks shy of his 32nd birthday. He took a shot in the throat and died in the street. He had two little girls, and his wife, Angie, is weeks away from delivering another baby.

On Friday, the afternoon of the guns, Angie Halcomb took her children to her mother's house, and when she returned in the evening, she turned on the television. There was a bulletin. A sniper, the TV announcer said, but he said it was in another district, not the Western. Angie Halcomb breathed a sigh of relief and went into the kitchen to make Easter eggs.

And then, a little later, she heard a knock on the front door.

"Angie," said a voice.

There were two of them standing there, two police who were friends of Jimmy, and Angie knew immediately that the worst thing in her life had happened.

"What are you here for?" she said.

"Open the door," one of them said.

She knew why they were there. She knew their faces, knew their uniforms, knew the sound in their voices. But she wouldn't let them in. Something in her head said, If I don't let them in, they won't tell me, and then Jimmy won't have to be dead.

"What are you here for?" she said again, knowing the answer, knowing it had to do with that sniper report she'd heard on the television.

"Please let us come in, Angie."

At Lombard and Carey Streets, they saw Jimmy Halcomb die in the street with television cameras carrying it into living rooms. In this neighborhood, random, pointless, bizarre violence is not exactly unique, but this had the modern McLuhanesque touch to it: the cameras whirring away, TV personalities thrusting microphones into witnesses' faces while it was happening, and neighborhood extras who kept wandering into the scene looking for roles to play amid the gunfire.

"Didja get on teevee?" a neighborhood girl asked the next morning. She looked 15 and held a cigarette between two fingers with the nails nubbed down. Her friend pouted. "My mother wouldn't let me outa the house."

And there it was: a chance in the limelight, and it had been blown. Around Lombard and Carey Streets, you don't get many of those chances. What you get is a lot of people doing drab, tough shift work in factories to pay for linoleum on their living room floors and furniture bought second hand. You get somebody selling dope in a hallway getting cut up by a couple of kids who want to express their dissatisfaction with his product. You get police nervously checking the alleys and the abandoned houses every night and trying to keep the bars quiet on the weekends.

All of this comes to a boil in one frustrated kid's head on an April evening, and he barricades himself well enough to give the television cameras time to move in and catch it for the folks at home.

In the morning, Angie Halcomb sat in her home with her children, Carrie, 6, and Jacqueline, 14 months. The young one wouldn't understand, but Angie had tried to tell Carrie that her father wouldn't be coming home again.

"She knows what heaven is," Angie Halcomb said now. "She knows it's a beautiful place."

"You said that's where her dad went?" somebody asked. Angie nodded her head.

"But she doesn't really understand what's happened," she said. "I'm afraid she still thinks Jimmy's gonna be home one night, and he's gonna walk through that door ... "

At Lombard and Carey, there was broken glass all over the street. In the morning heat, a few neighborhood people were trying to sweep it up while others, the sightseers, were out pointing fingers.

"When I got up this morning, I had to look at the house again to make sure it wasn't a dream," said Harry Lawhorn. He sat on his front steps, directly across from the gunfire site and told a TV crew what had happened. He told them about his friend John Earl Williams, who was charged in the shooting, about a kid who kept to himself most of the time, a kid who bottled up his frustrations, who'd quietly put away an arsenal in the bedroom of his parents' little row house apartment and then decided to use it all one night.

When the TV people went away, some of his friends gently taunted Harry about being a television celebrity and a big shot.

"I'm just doing it for Johnny's sake," Harry said, flipping his hand as though swatting away a fly. "Somebody's gotta stick up for the boy."

Across the street, John Earl Williams's parents sat behind heavy green curtains in a darkened living room. Every time a reporter came to the door, a woman would open it and say, slightly self-consciously, "I'm sorry, no comment."

"Yeah, they really busted the place up last night," Harry Lawhorn was saying now. "Knocked the furniture all over the place, and records lying all over the floor. They really made a mess."

"The police?" somebody asked.

"Yeah, the police. What did they have to mess up the house for?"

"After they took Johnny to jail," somebody said, "all the TV cameras wanted to get into the house to take pictures. But Johnny's mother wouldn't even let 'em."

"Damn right," Harry Lawhorn said. "I wouldn't want anybody coming in my house when it looked like that, neither."

APRIL 10, 1976

ODDS CATCH UP WITH "CROWBAR"

"Come over here," says Dominic "Crowbar" Carozza, appearing somewhat more confident than expected at the occasion of his own murder trial.

"Me?" says a man at the rear of Judge Hillary Caplan's criminal courtroom.

"You," says Carozza.

He's sitting at the defense table during a lull in the legal action, and waves one meaty arm like a traffic cop at Calvert and Fayette.

"How's our friend the bookmaker?" Carozza asks the man at closer range.

"Good. Real good."

"That's good," says Carozza, feeling flush with confidence even as prosecutors outline this case that could send him away for the rest of his life. "Tell him something for me. Tell him it's six-to-five this jury finds me innocent."

"Six-to-five?" the man asks, contemplating such odds. "That's it?"

Carozza thinks about this for a moment. He glances at his codefendant, Robert "Tattoo Bobby" Vizzini. Now he gazes above, not to the courtroom ceiling, but to heaven beyond, where inspiration is due at any moment.

"Wait a minute," he says now, getting a vision and rubbing his forehead like Carnac the Magnificent. He voice carries across this entire court. "Wait a minute. Nine-to-two. That's it, nine-to-two I'm walking. 'Cause it's damn sure I ain't getting a conviction."

That was a couple of days ago. On Tuesday, a few days after Crowbar Carozza sat there in Baltimore Circuit Court making book on the outcome of his own life, a jury disagreed with him. They found both Carozza and Vizzini guilty in the murder of a junkie named Russell Charles Baker last June 22 on Pier Seven of the Fells Point waterfront, and the odds on Crowbar dropped off the table altogether.

The murder was classic street business. Prosecutors say Carozza loaned money to Baker and Marsha Hammons, who was Crowbar's girlfriend, to buy heroin in Brooklyn, New York. Baker and Hammons were to come back to Baltimore and sell the stuff at a nice profit.

Slight problem: Hammons, Baker, and Baker's girlfriend, Deana Bishop, used all the heroin themselves before they made it back to Baltimore, and then tried to tell Carozza they got burned in Brooklyn. The next thing anybody knew, Baker had six bullets in him.

That's the way it was told in court, anyway. A parade of witnesses—described by defense attorney Philip Sutley as "drug addicts, psychopaths, alcoholics, habitual liars"—told of Carozza and Vizzini getting rid of Russell Charles Baker. Some of these witnesses made deals with prosecutors to go easy on their own cases. Sutley called this "sickening," as though he'd never in his life seen the likes of it.

"All the promises made to this bunch of degenerates," Crowbar Carozza complained during a trial break. "Just so they can get me, they let
everybody else go. All these deals."

"Monte Hall," said a bemused court officer. "*Let's Make A Deal.*"

"I like that analysis," said Carozza, nodding his head appreciatively.

"Don't quote me," said the officer.

"You can quote me," said Carozza. "I like it."

But he didn't like it two days ago, when prosecutor Timothy J. Doory
stood in front of the jury and explained the way real life is conducted
in the courts of law these days. Deals? Of course there are deals.

"Sometimes you have to let the little fish go to catch the big
fish," said Doory. "The fish that was caught was a shark."

He meant Carozza. For several decades in Crowbar's life now, murder charges came and usually went. Guys got beat up and Crowbar took
on a reputation. Some said he dangled a guy off the Bay Bridge because
the guy owed money. Crowbar said, nah, he never worked the bridge.
Some said he drove a truck through a bar because somebody else owed
him money. Crowbar let the story circulate long enough to add to his
legend. One guy Crowbar admitted shooting, but that was because the
guy came at him with a club.

Finally, somebody got even with Carozza by blowing up his car one
morning. Crowbar was in it. He lost a leg in the explosion but never
complained.

"I never asked who did it," he explained over lunch one day not long
ago. "When you play the game, you don't complain."

And the legend grew. One thing the legend never included, though,
was drugs. Carozza, 59, comes from a different generation of street
guys, a different set of ground rules. Playing tough was one thing; making money off needles in arms was something else.

"Come on," he said during a break in his trial, "everybody knows
me better than that. Me and drugs? No way. What am I, a total
idiot?"

But there is no denying this: The people in his girlfriend's life, and
those on the fringes of his own life, were more and more involved with
the drug trade. Usually, junkies' lives get pretty sloppy. Sometimes, they
take hostages.

On Albemarle Street, in Little Italy, there has long been a sign on the
sidewalk outside Crowbar Carozza's home. In a neighborhood legend-

ary for its lack of parking spaces, the sign says: Reserved for Dominic Carozza. And nobody who knew the name ever dared park there.

"You can use my space," Carozza said two days ago. "It should be unoccupied for a while."

MARCH 7, 1991

MESSAGE TO D.C.: DRUG WAR LOST

Her name was Posie, and we put the verb in the past tense under advisement.

Posie used to come into the barbershop that isn't there any more at Greenmount and North Avenues. She was a heroin addict before anybody in power wanted to talk about heroin addicts. It was 20 years ago, and Posie would stumble into the barbershop, where the numbers runners and the crap shooters and the street hustlers hung out, and she'd ask if anybody wanted to go back to her room.

This morning, the mayor of Baltimore takes a trip to Washington to talk about the people like Posie who may still be among the living, but only if we are talking technically.

In the barbershop even back then, men turned their heads away from Posie. She wore dresses that hung randomly off her wasted body. Up and down her arms were blackened holes, the puncture-mark residue of years of needle abuse. The guys in the barbershop would throw a few bucks Posie's way, but I never saw any of them who wanted to go home with her.

It didn't matter to her. She'd take the few dollars from the barbershop, and she'd go to this guy up on the corner, and the guy had dope to sell, and Posie would somehow escape through another day.

And in that time in South Baltimore, in a place called Cherry Hill, the reflections of Posie were everywhere, junkies wandering dazed through the street looking for something to put in their veins.

In the lot behind St. Veronica's Church one night, there were two of them I knew pretty well, explaining the psychology of sustaining a drug habit.

"Got that woman's refrigerator," one of them said. "Knocked on the front door, nobody home, so then I just slipped around the back window and got in and walked out the front door with it."

"But how do you get away with it?" I asked.

"Just walk down the street with it," said the other one. "People look at you and say, 'Look at that fool out there, walking down the street with a refrigerator.'"

"That's right," said the first. "Just act like you belong."

An entire subculture was just beginning its primordial crawl onto land, and nobody in power wanted to admit it was happening: drug addicts breaking into houses, knocking down old ladies, turning tricks in barbershops to support their habits.

Now, nobody wants to believe it's gotten bad enough to talk about decriminalizing drugs. We're always 20 years behind the curve. The mayor of Baltimore, Kurt L. Schmoke, heads to Capitol Hill to say we've got to change course, and all around are voices screaming bloody murder at him.

Twenty years ago, a federal prosecutor called in one of this city's honest criminals, an East Baltimore numbers operator later driven out of business when the state of Maryland decided to enter his line of work.

"Why are you worried about a little gambling?" the bookmaker asked. "Why aren't you doing something about these junkies out there?"

"What junkies?" the prosecutor asked. "It's only in the deep ghetto. There's no narcotics in the white neighborhoods."

The prosecutor didn't want to believe it, nor did the deep thinkers at city hall. One of them heard about the drug traffic in Cherry Hill and said, "What the hell, Cherry Hill, it's way over on the other side of the Hanover Street Bridge."

Out of sight, out of mind. The city police commissioner in that time was named Donald Pomerleau. His police kept telling him of more and more dope cases. The junkies were committing all these crimes, the street cops said. Pomerleau brushed them off, told them he already had a narcotics unit.

He was right. There were a dozen cops in this unit. A dozen cops, while the junkie population multiplied by the thousands all around them and the street cops didn't know where to turn first.

And now the mayor of Baltimore says the whole damned country has lost its sense of direction. He talks of decriminalizing drugs. He goes onto Ted Koppel's show at night, and he visits cities, and frankly the response out there isn't wonderful.

In Washington, he presents his case formally. Decriminalize drugs, he says, and focus on treatment of addicts, or the nation will continue to become the captive of these people.

This is the voice of frustration talking. For 20 years, the country has tried to look the other way. They thought it was only the people like Posie, or the guys in ghettos like Cherry Hill, or maybe white teenagers going through a brief flirtation with the unknown.

But the drug traffic took on a life of its own, and it's made daily existence in American cities very dangerous. We can't imprison our way out of it, and we can't go on living this way.

And that's all the mayor of Baltimore is saying.

SEPTEMBER 29, 1988

TAKING PLASTIC ON THE BLOCK

In the summer of 1987, by his own admission, Michael J. Gianakos went to a nightclub on The Block and ordered one prostitute. And it was good.

It was so good that, as the summer progressed, Gianakos went to more nightclubs on The Block and ordered more prostitutes, and then more and more. This was good for Gianakos not only because he was having a swell sexual fling, but because he wasn't paying a cent for any of it.

American Express was footing the bill.

Every time Gianakos hired a prostitute at one of these clubs, he simply pulled out his American Express card and said, "Charge it." In a highly athletic two-month period, he said these words to the tune of $6,716.92—of which, over the past 20 months, he has paid American Express exactly nothing.

And so, in Baltimore Circuit Court, we now have American Express suing Gianakos for its money, and Gianakos refusing on the most remarkable grounds, to wit:

    a. He spent the money on prostitutes.
    b. Prostitution is illegal.
    c. Any contract that involves illegal actions cannot
       be enforced.

Does this man stay up nights figuring angles, or what?

In a complaint filed in circuit court, American Express bluntly declares, "The defendant has no defense."

But, in a response to that complaint filed by attorney Thomas Waxter Jr., the former city councilman now with the law firm of Semmes, Bowen & Semmes, Gianakos not only declares American Express is out of luck, but also asks the court to award him money for having to put up with all this lawsuit nonsense.

Meanwhile, no nightclub owners on The Block have filed court papers, although an employee at the Club Pussycat said yesterday, "Prostitution? There's no prostitution on The Block. Where do people get these ideas?"

This will come as a shock to Gianakos, an assembly line worker from Northeast Baltimore, who claims to have run up his $6,716.92 bill at three clubs on The Block during July and August of 1987.

"American Express is a big boy," says attorney Waxter. "They have to answer for dealing with The Block. If they send their salespeople there to open accounts, then they have to take the risk, like anybody else on The Block. This isn't a frivolous defense. This is Maryland law."

Which, briefly put, is this:

—*Baxter vs. Wilburn,* in which the Maryland Court of Appeals held that "contracts based upon the consideration . . . of illicit sexual intercourse . . . are void and unenforceable."

—*Donovan vs. Scuderi,* in which the same high court ruled that a contract cannot be enforceable "if its only purpose is sexual relationship for hire."

Of this, Waxter drily notes in court papers, "There can be no question that Michael Gianakos's visits to many different women, over a short period of time, at bars located on The Block, was not motivated by a romance worthy of Romeo and Juliet."

American Express says this willfully misses the point. Its contract with Gianakos was legal, and his business with prostitutes is strictly secondary.

"Look, we're in two and a half million places around the world," says Gary Tobin, American Express vice president of public affairs. "We're in 150 countries. We can't check out every single place that accepts the cards. If they violate the law in these clubs, we assume you have police and courts in Baltimore. We don't police these places, and we can't judge what goes on in them."

Tough luck, says defense attorney Waxter.

"It'd be the same thing if it was a gambling debt," he says, neatly overlooking the fact that not many gambling operations accept American Express. "Anybody with an illegal debt takes a risk, and American Express is no different from anybody else."

One slight problem: When he rented his ladies of the evening, Gianakos's bills didn't exactly specify prostitutes. They said "champagne," which is not illegal in the state of Maryland.

For their part, proprietors on The Block continue to say that Gianakos is full of baloney.

"In the first place," one club owner said yesterday, "we don't allow prostitution here. And, in the second place, we never take credit cards for it."

MARCH 9, 1989

A MURDERER'S MOTHER

The guards are leading him into the courthouse, in handcuffs, when his family turns the corner just in time to wave to him.

"We'll see you inside, hon," the wife calls out.

"Good luck," the sister cries.

"He's a good boy," the mother explains. "He's just troubled."

Her son was convicted of murder. He and a friend, both high on drugs, fought with a third man, and a death took place. That's how the mother describes it: A death took place. A verbal distance is created, to be followed by an emotional distance. It's as though her son happened along and there was an errant knife that turned out to be attached to his hand plunging into a wayward body and, what do you know, a death took place.

The son is here to be sentenced. Judges listen to verbal distancing but pay attention to facts. Families arrive to put emotions around those facts.

Thus, here is the father, a rail-like, bony man with his hat in his hand, glowering darkly as he stands by himself in the hallway outside court; the mother, squat, wringing her hands as she rests on a bench, a large puddle of a woman; the defendant's young wife, blond hair parted in the middle like theater curtains, trying hard to cover all wayward emotions; and the sister, in her late teens, who has brought her two-year-old daughter along, all dressed up to say goodbye to her uncle.

The mother folds her hands across her belly, idly turning her thumbs.

"My son is not what came out at the trial," she says. "His bad moments were five or six times in his life."

"Oh, Ma," the daughter says.

"He was sick," the mother says. "He wouldn't tell me what it was, but he said he was sick and it would take time to cure. And then he would go to his room alone, or he'd walk the streets by himself on the coldest nights, just to get away from people."

"Ma," the daughter says, nodding toward a reporter, "he's not interested in that."

For a moment, the mother ceases talking. A death took place, that's all she knows. Why is her son in court just because a death took place?

"I can remember him going to the aid of a wounded squirrel," she says now. "My God, the things a mother remembers. Things he probably forgot about himself."

"Ma," the daughter says. Of them all, she seems the only one vaguely embarrassed. The others have adopted defense mechanisms: Some cosmic mistake has been made, they seem to imply.

Inside court, they are given a moment with the boy. He is 22 and has deep, dark, jailbird eyes. The mother and wife kiss him gently. The sister tells him, "You look like a greaser."

The father stands a few feet behind them and points to his son.

"Pretty nice looking, huh?"

"Huh?"

"Nice-looking guy, huh?"

In minutes, the mother is called to say a few words. The son sits next to his attorney and looks uncomfortable at the sight of his mother: a woman, after all, taking up for a man. A few rows back, the young wife clutches hands with her sister-in-law.

"I'm sorry," she whispers. "I always get the shakes."

"My son," the mother tells the judge now, "is not what came out at the trial." She goes on to tell about the mystery sickness that turned out to be drugs, of the son walking the streets by himself, as though these stories told in the hall moments earlier were a dress rehearsal for this courtroom plea.

"I would hear him crying at night," the mother says, "telling his father, 'Dad, I have no place to go but up.' "

The young wife shakes visibly. The father blows his nose into a handkerchief. A death took place, but their boy had problems of his own. The sister looks around, hoping no familiar faces are in the room.

"He's always been reaching out," the father tells the judge a few moments later. "He's always been running. One time when we were living down the county, I saw him standing on a hillside. I stopped the car right on the highway. I just grabbed him and hugged him.

"He's not a bad boy, judge," the father says. He pauses, looking for some magic explanation. "He's just emotional. And I'm the emotional father."

And he retreats to his seat now, trying vainly to hold back tears. He and his son embrace for a moment, and the father lets out a loud, painful sob that fills the courtroom.

"Do you have any final words before sentencing?" the judge asks.

The moment seems to have sprung upon the son a little unexpectedly, he's been so absorbed by what has been said. A piece of him is still holding onto that embrace of the father. But the son looks down at his hands now, and begins to talk in a voice just above a whisper.

"I'm sorry the man's dead," he says, "and I'm sorry I've hurt my family so much." A clock on a rear wall moves a few ticks in the courtroom silence. "And there was some testimony during the trial that I didn't get along with my father. Well, I worship my father."

The sound of a deep-throated sob fills the room once again, and then again and again. The mother clutches rosary beads and leans her head onto the bench in front of her. The young wife is trembling in her seat.

The judge says he sympathizes with the family, but he has no alternative. He calls it the typical end of a life in drugs: people wounded everywhere. The son will do 20 years. He leaves the courtroom glancing over his shoulder at his family.

"He's a good boy," the father says.

"My son didn't want to kill anybody," the mother says.

"Ma," says the daughter, looking around a little distractedly. "Nobody wants to hear that."

OCTOBER 8, 1989

THE LOGIC OF LARCENY

On Eastern Avenue, Anton the Thief displays his latest bit of business, a three-foot-high statue of an anciently garbed man, which seems to have been made of some highly impressive imitation marble.

"You know who this is?" Anton the Thief asks yesterday.

"Somebody famous?" a guy says.

"St. Francis of Assisi," Anton the Thief declares with religious fervor.

"You stole a saint?"

"Not stole," Anton corrects. "Kidnapped him. Now I'm offering him for ransom."

A gentle breeze wafts its way up Eastern Avenue, and so does Anton's gaze. He's looking for customers, preferably religious souls with money to spend. Standing beside Anton the Thief is his wife, who confirms that the statue is, indeed, St. Francis. She is considered the religious one in the family, having attended Sunday school once in her youth. The wife's name is Dora, although for formal newspaper interviews she is known as Mrs. Thief.

"But this is a saint," a second guy says to Anton. "It's a holy man. You can't go around swiping holy men."

"Wrong," Anton quickly asserts. He looks a little sensitive about this, a little defensive, a man braced in advance for a certain onslaught of disapproval. "See," he says, "I've looked into this thing. You look at your Bible, you'll see."

"Bible?"

"Bible," says Anton. "Ain't nothing in the Bible about one kind of stealing being worse than another kind of stealing. It just says stealing. The Bible doesn't say, 'Stealing a TV set is bad, but stealing a statue of a saint is worse.' Stealing's just stealing, so what's the difference?"

In a world where morality is on permanent leave, this is logic to live by. For the last decade now, Anton and Mrs. Thief have been stealing with missionary fervor to support their drug habits. In a city with tens of thousands of addicts, this makes them part of a large and predatory army.

About 21 thousand persons a year are convicted of crimes in this city. The cops estimate that about 75 percent of all crime is drug related, a figure that involves thievery of all kinds. In this climate, is anyone surprised that an occasional religious figure is among the casualties?

The statue of St. Francis is actually quite lovely. Anton the Thief holds it up and suggests running your hands over it. It's an off-white imitation marble, with a couple of birds perched atop the shoulders of the 13th-century saint known for his love of nature and animals.

"Gotta be $300," Anton the Thief says.

"You think you're gonna get $300 for this?" he's asked.

"No, I'll settle for $70," he says. "But it's worth $300. That's what the store wanted for it."

No way, he is told, are people going to buy a stolen saint.

"No way?" says Anton.

"No way."

But now, on Eastern Avenue, a remarkable thing begins to happen. People appear out of buildings and begin to examine St. Francis. They admire the fine workmanship, the beatific look on the face of the statue, the graceful sweep of the fine imitation marble.

In their admiration, everyone talks price and no one talks ethics.

"Look at them birds," says a woman pushing a little shopping basket. "St. Francis liked them birds, didn't he?"

"I think he was their patron saint," says Anton the Thief. "If you read your Bible."

St. Francis having lived long after the New Testament was written, this is misleading but not entirely misguided. St. Francis's love of nature is one of his best-remembered characteristics, and he is generally represented in art as surrounded by animals, a fact that Anton the Thief cares about not even slightly.

"Is that marble," a man in a checkered sports coat asks, "or is it ivory?"

"Not real marble, I wouldn't think," says Anton's wife, Mrs. Thief, attempting to show a little honesty. "But it's a quality piece of work."

Behind the man in the sports coat and the woman with the shopping basket come more potential buyers, one after the other, all admiring the sculpture, and none asking about the conditions under which St.

Francis of Assisi winds up on Eastern Avenue during the lunch hour.

"Where is it? Where is it?" a woman in a white waitress outfit cries now, rushing up to see the statue. She takes one glance, and a wave of disappointment washes over her face.

"Oh," she says sadly, running her hands over the figure. "It's St. Francis you're selling. I heard it was the Holy Mother."

It goes this way for maybe 20 minutes. Everybody's interested, but nobody quite has $70 to put together for a statue, even if it does mean rescuing St. Francis from his kidnappers.

Times are tough, and money is scarce. Also, things being how they are, Anton the Thief is getting a little nervous about the police and wishes to change location.

"What'll you do," he's asked, "if you can't find a buyer?"

"I don't know," he says. "Maybe sell it to some priest."

AUGUST 29, 1991

PUBLIC DEFENDER

Alan Murrell says he's retiring, but I don't want to believe it. The man's only 88 years old. Whoever heard of retiring in the prime of your life?

"I feel that way, too," Murrell admitted yesterday. "But I reached a point where I guess I've antagonized everybody, so it's time to go."

Did somebody say antagonize?

Murrell is Maryland's chief public defender. Every year, he battles the state legislature for more money so his office can defend clients the rest of the world wants to cremate on the spot. The legislators think he's a pain. Murrell thinks the legislators are constitutional cretins.

"Morons," he calls them with a certain gladiatorial glee in his voice. "I'm dealing with a bunch of morons. Would you yourself look to any member of the legislature to represent you? Let's be frank about it. You'd be sure they'd sell you down the river at some point, wouldn't you?"

Did somebody say antagonize?

Some years back, a city judge sent Murrell a letter complaining that public defender staff attorneys were hanging their coats in the judge's outer office and using his private toilet facilities.

Murrell sent back a terse response: The attorneys used the judge's office for their coats because they'd be stolen if they left them in the courtroom. As for the toilets, Murrell's staff would no longer use the judge's chambers. They'd use the windows.

Antagonize?

Once, in court, Murrell muttered something in an opposing attorney's ear.

"Your honor," the attorney cried, "Mr. Murrell just called me a rotten [expletive deleted]."

Murrell looked at the judge with all the innocence of a choirboy.

"I didn't say a word, your honor," he declared. "Maybe he read my mind."

Once, Murrell defended a gambling figure the cops said they'd picked up on a telephone wiretap. The cops said he was taking bets on races at Hialeah. Murrell smelled a rat.

"Hialeah?" he asked in court.

"Yes, sir," testified a vice squad cop on the witness stand.

"That's a lie," said Murrell, looking at the date on the police warrant. "Hialeah wasn't even running that week."

The cops had simply made up the conversation that was the basis for their arrest. He caught them doing it another time, when they alleged they'd picked up conversations from a telephone inside a bar. Again, Murrell checked the date on the warrant. It happened to be Election Day. All the bars were closed.

When Murrell worked a case, normally blasé courthouse types would leave the corridors and pile into the room to watch him strut his stuff. Once, before the public defender's office existed, a judge spotted him in District Court, pointed to an indigent man, and said, "You're this man's attorney. Take five minutes to talk to him and prepare him for trial."

Murrell replied, "This man doesn't need a lawyer; he needs a priest."

Also, though, he needed a lawyer. People keep getting arrested who happen to be poor. This means they can't afford an attorney to represent them, and there's a certain Sixth Amendment to the U.S. Constitution saying poor people have the same right to competent legal defense as people with money.

That's where Murrell comes in. As chief of the public defender's office since 1971, his duties have been mostly administrative, but his battles have been legendary.

In the beginning, critics said poor people should hire a lawyer just like everybody else. Even defendants complained. "Get me a real lawyer," they'd say. The "real" lawyers—the private attorneys who made their living off criminals who had money—hated the office, too. They said the public defenders would monopolize all the defendants. There wouldn't be enough criminals to go around.

They must have been dreaming.

About 100 thousand criminals turn to the public defender's office each year, and there are still untapped thousands more who turn to private attorneys. Without the public defender's office, the system would choke on its own abundance.

And yet, every year, Murrell advances on Annapolis to battle over money. The legislature says: No more. Murrell says: Whether you give me money or not, I'm still gonna spend it, only I'll send you the bill in the mail.

The battles are behind him now, though he says he's not really retiring. "What am I gonna do?" he said yesterday. "Play dead?"

At his age? Come on, the guy's in the midst of his very own legend.

APRIL 24, 1990

THE NIGHT THEY BUSTED AL ISELLA

On the night of October 29, with nothing better to do in their gallant fight against crime, half a dozen police crashed into the house where Albert Isella sat with his wife and daughter and two grandchildren.

With guns drawn and all ears ignoring the cries of the frightened children, the police then arrested Isella, who is 78 years old. The charge? Taking bets on two college football games.

Does everybody feel safer now? The homicide rate breaks all records, and the junkies are knocking over old ladies for their bingo money, and you roll the dice with your children's lives when you send them onto the street, but somehow the cops find time for 78-year-old men who might be taking a football bet?

Let's be clear about something here: Al Isella is no choirboy and doesn't pretend to be. Over the years, the record makes very clear, he has done his share of bookmaking, and then some.

"How many times," he was asked yesterday, outside a criminal court-room, "have you been arrested over the years."

"Fifty-two times," he said in a voice that rang like brass bands down the courthouse corridor.

"Fifty-two?"

"Well, yeah," he said. "Not counting, you know, street fights when I was a kid and stuff."

OK, we got that out of the way. His life is no chamber of commerce brochure, and sometimes it has taken on certain comic effects in the pursuit of a dollar. One night he stepped out of a phone booth and was confronted by a city cop.

"Hello, Al," the officer said.

"Hello, Sarge," Al replied.

"Al," the officer asked, "you still taking bets on horses?"

"No, Sarge," said Al, "I quit."

"Can I search you?"

"Sure."

In one pocket, the policeman found a small notebook with names and telephone numbers. Then he found a slip with $135 worth of play. Then a slip with the names of 10 racehorses.

"I changed my mind," said Al, shoving the cop away. "I don't want you to search me now."

The cop went on to find a scratch sheet and some more money, and the incident wound up in the newspapers. Big deal. People see a head-line and reach for a conclusion of great racketeering. Some years back, the cops picked up an address book of Al's, and in it were the names of 11 American League baseball umpires. The credibility of the American pastime teetered.

It was nothing, Al explained. The book merely served as his Christ-mas card list, and the umps were simply his friends. Absolutely every-body in law enforcement figured he was lying.

"I never booked a baseball bet in my life," Al said. "If I'm guilty of something wrong with the umpires, then the pope is guilty. I would never embarrass them guys."

He told the truth. The FBI investigated, and the baseball commission-er's office investigated, and when it was over, everybody cleared him.

For Isella, it represented a kind of double victory, at once declaring him innocent while adding to his legend. For several decades around here, he's been some people's model of a classic mobster, fully equipped with brave talk, broken syntax, and an Italian name.

Al's never tried to discourage this kind of talk, even when he knew some of it was crazy. It added to his street stature. He'd stand on Albemarle Street in Little Italy, and he'd open the trunk of his car for people to see a treasury of items. The stuff was intended to look like hot merchandise. Al knew about that element of human nature that puts a little larceny in people's souls.

He'd buy the stuff at Andrews Wholesale Warehouse, at Albemarle and Fleet, or pick it up cheap from a nylon stocking company, or buy it at goverment tax auctions.

It was his version of a supplemental income: the selling of wholesale goods to help out a gambling livelihood that, in recent years, was going away. The reason was simple. The state of Maryland, in bringing us a lottery and El Gordo and Keno games and so forth, has now virtually monopolized a business that once gave Al Isella a living.

So now, the cops have him taking football bets. They charged into his house last October and found evidence of bets on two college games.

"Judge," said Isella's attorney, Richard Karceski, "in all fairness, it happens every weekend all over this country. Millions of people betting on ballgames."

"Doesn't make it right," declared Judge Charles Foos.

Isella drummed his fingers heavily on a defense table and shifted in his seat. Somebody said he could be in jail for Christmas.

"So I'll be in jail," said Isella, voice booming across the courtroom. "Big deal. So I'll save money on some Christmas gifts."

After all this time, he's learned not to take this courtroom business too seriously. Too bad the courts can't do the same. Judge Foos fined him $500 and gave him a year's probation. Haven't these people heard there's real crime out there they should be fighting?

DECEMBER 24, 1992

BAD MEN MAKE THE MOST OF BAD SITUATIONS

That day on North Carey Street, the cops charged into the room in mid-rape. The girl was pinned down on a pile of dirty rags, screaming madly. She was 16 and slender. The guy, 28 years old, broad and muscular, wore nothing but a shirt.

"Get off me," the girl cried. "Help, get off me, no, no!" In all the noise, neither she nor the guy heard the cops come into the room until the first one, Officer Victor Gearhart of the Western District, stood over them and asked, almost flippantly, "Is there a problem here?"

"Officers," said the man, jumping to his feet, "this is my girlfriend. We do this a lot. Don't believe a word she says."

On the pile of rags, the girl sobbed and looked for something to cover herself.

"Hon, are you OK?" Gearhart asked now.

"No."

"Is this your boyfriend?"

"No, it's not my boyfriend. He raped me."

This was in July of '87. In the Baltimore courthouse, prosecutors looked at the guy's previous record. He had 40 arrests and 18 convictions, including assault with a deadly weapon, assaulting police, receiving stolen goods, and malicious destruction of property.

Also, there were three previous rape arrests—though, in each case, he'd beaten the charges and they couldn't be introduced as evidence when the Carey Street case came to trial last March.

Officers Gearhart and Todd Eidner took the stand that day and ran through the entire scenario. The 16-year-old girl did the same. Then came the defendant, who immediately changed his story.

Well, no, she wasn't really his girlfriend, he said. She was just a girl who'd agreed to have sex with him in exchange for money and drugs. He said she'd put the money in her blouse. But the police said there was no money in her blouse, and there were no drugs anywhere on the premises.

The case took two days. The jury took 90 minutes. Not guilty on all counts. For the fourth time, the guy had beaten a rape charge.

"She was a very nice girl," assistant state's attorney Joan Bossman said at the time, "but very inarticulate. And from a bad neighborhood. And the jury seemed to be very affected by that. I've never seen anything like it."

Now she has. At 11:30 the other night, a 37-year-old woman sat in her boyfriend's living room on North Avenue. They were drinking heavily. There was a knock on the door. When the woman opened it, the man outside grabbed her, pulled her outside, and pushed her into a car before the boyfriend could react.

The man drove her one block up North Avenue and took her into his apartment. Inside were several other men. For the next few hours, the men took sexual turns with her.

Toward dawn, the men fell asleep. The woman started to climb out a window. "Don't do that," one of the men said. "It's the second floor."

"I want to get out of here," the woman said.

The man opened the door and let her go. She ran home, called the police, and took them to the apartment where she'd been attacked. Standing out front was the man who'd first abducted her.

Two days later, the case was given to Joan Bossman at the state's attorney's office. When she saw the defendant, she couldn't believe her eyes.

It was the man the cops had caught in mid-rape on North Carey Street the summer before.

"My first thought," Bossman said yesterday, "was, 'I knew it was going to happen again.' I just didn't think it would be this soon."

Bossman questioned the woman at length. She said she'd been kept in a locked bedroom on North Avenue, said she'd screamed for a while until the man who'd abducted her hit her in the face and threatened to kill her if she didn't stop.

Bossman looked at the woman's face: one eye was swollen and bruised and there were cuts in the skin.

But there was a problem. The woman admitted she'd been drinking, and her memory wasn't sharp. First, she said there were five men in the apartment. Then, four. Then, three. She thought there had been two men in the car when she was abducted, but her boyfriend remembered seeing only one.

"My difficulty," Bossman said, "was the gaps in her memory. Not knowing how many men had raped her, not remembering how many were in the car. I believe every word she said, but I knew I'd have a problem in court. I liked the fact that she was honest with me. She admitted she'd been drinking and she was high. She'd admitted she didn't remember certain things. Some women will shade details. She didn't. She was very open. And there's absolutely no doubt in my mind she was telling me the truth."

But there is truth, and there is truth that will stand up in court.

Bossman had no other witnesses, and no other evidence. Thus, she had no choice. A few days ago, the case was dismissed. The woman simply wasn't a good enough witness.

"He knows who to pick," a frustrated Bossman said of the woman's abductor. "The situations show he always picks the most vulnerable victims—unemployed, poor, inarticulate women, women who are frightened of the legal system."

And now he has been charged with raping five women, and in all five cases, he has beaten the rap.

JULY 8, 1987

KIDS

Putting a Hold on

Time Itself

Sometimes it's not so easy being a child in this city.

A lot of the kids today come from broken homes, where the parents are absent physically, or might as well be. Drive down too many city streets and see the evidence: There's school the next day, and it's 11 at night and children are out there by the score.

Teenage pregnancy is among the highest in the nation, giving ammunition to the cynics who call this "The City That Breeds." Or, considering the children shot in random gunplay, "The City That Bleeds."

The public schools are rough and seriously underfunded, and a lot of kids, taking matters into their own hands absent anyone else's, finally opt not to show up at all. It's routine in many schools for a class to enter ninth grade and graduate, four years later, with more than half of its original members having dropped out somewhere along the way.

But it's also true that the city experience gives kids a strength of character you can't invent out in suburbia. They're exposed to the American experience we used to call the melting pot.

And some of them lift the hearts of all who are around them.

BUILDING ON SUBTLE PLEASURES

Ah, the subtle pleasures of little league baseball.

See the routine ground ball hit to the second baseman of the Northwest Little Indians, who is poised and alert and moves with infinite grace. Now see the routine ground ball going through the second baseman's legs and into right field. The right fielder is backing up the second baseman. He comes charging in with a sprinter's speed. Now see the ball going through his legs, too.

While this is going on, marvelous things are happening here and there: The batter has commenced running around the bases. The first baseman is practicing his golf swing. The third baseman is engaged in a high-level conversation with himself. The shortstop is trying to yank out a loose front tooth. The left fielder is having his quiet time.

Now the right fielder has galloped after the ball, picked it up, and flung it back to the second baseman, who whips around gracefully and fires a thing of beauty, a rainbow of a throw, an absolute strike, completely over the backstop.

On the sidelines, Sam Zervitz should be having an anxiety attack. He's coach of these Northwest Indians, this team that has won all but 12 of its 14 games this year. For a living, Zervitz is a public information officer for the city's public schools. Some think this is a pretty tough job. They should watch him coach little league.

Zervitz started his coaching chores last spring, apparently in his right mind, at the annual league player draft. At this draft, coaches from each of the six league teams took turns selecting players on the basis of playing skills and other subtle factors.

"We had scouting reports," Zervitz smiles, "with information like, 'This player's sensitive. You can't yell at him. You yell at him, he wets his pants.' Or, 'This kid daydreams and he runs to the ice cream truck between innings.' Or, 'This kid's father will drive you crazy.' Or, 'This kid cries.' But that's nothing unusual. All the kids have cried at least once."

Probably, so have the coaches. Consider a few opportunities.

"One of our guys hit an inside-the-park home run," Zervitz says, "but all four of our runners landed on home plate at the same time, all tangled up in their slides, and the ball got there the same instant." The catcher, not knowing who to tag, simply tagged out everybody.

"Any ball hit to the outfield," Zervitz laughs, "becomes Shakespearean tragedy. I haven't seen an outfield catch all year. If it gets hit to the outfield, it's a home run. One kid lost the ball in the grass and couldn't find it for 10 minutes."

There are coaches who would get frustrated over this. There are leagues where 10-year-olds with limited ability would wallow on the bench. There are grownups who take little league baseball too seriously.

"The thing everybody around here tries to keep in mind," says Zervitz, "is that this is a kid activity, supervised by grownups. Not an adult activity with kids as pawns."

Also, as he sees it, it's a metaphor for a few things happening in Northwest Baltimore. "Community stabilization," says Zervitz. "We bring out parents who have mutual concerns—their kids—over a period of several months, and they get involved with each other and with their community. It's a demographic composite, with every professional level, every ethnic group, every educational and socioeconomic level. It's a good, solid, valuable thing that needs to be built on."

Of course, any team with a 2-and-12 record needs to build on a lot of things. But Zervitz has his excuses. He had a center fielder who positioned himself on Seven Mile Lane. He had a right fielder who climbed the outfield fence a lot. He lost some games by breathtakingly close scores.

Like 27 to 8.

And 34 to 9.

Also, he should have had more girls on the team. "There are only two in the league," he says. "One of them is on the first-place team, which is coached by Mrs. [Janet] Seidel. The girl's name is Tova, and you can't get her out. She's real small, and she walks every time. We had the other girl, but she fell out of a tree and broke her arm. It was too bad. Don't spread this around, but she looked like she was better than a lot of the boys."

It's been that kind of a season.

ALI DELIVERS LOW BLOW

Muhammad Ali took one look at Steven Yellity and tried to hit him with a punch. Is he crazy? Everybody knows you don't hit a guy with glasses. What's worse, he hit Yellity below the belt.

Ali, the former heavyweight champ of the world, showed up at Douglass High School yesterday, allegedly to talk about world hunger. Yellity, 17, an 11th-grader who wears thick glasses and has a weight problem, showed up in the school auditorium and called his bluff.

In front of adoring kids at Douglass, Ali boasted of being "the greatest of all time." He made a few lame jokes. Steven Yellity began to shift around in his auditorium seat.

Then Ali introduced a few friends from the entertainment world. One made some tasteless jokes about Michael Jackson. Another did Stevie Wonder impressions. Yellity sat there wondering what this had to do with world hunger.

Then Muhammad Ali took questions from the audience:

"Can I come up and give you a kiss?" one girl asked.

"How did you first get started in show business?" asked another.

Then one girl said, "How does this world hunger organization of yours work?"

And Muhammad Ali replied, "How come you look so serious? How come you're pointing your finger at me?"

The audience laughed, and the girl sat down in embarrassment.

Then Ali put on a tape recording of himself singing a song. In the audience, a student named Anthony Brown, 17, a 12th-grader, leaned toward his English teacher, Madeline Topkins, and said, "This seems phony. They ain't saying nothing. How come they ain't talking about hunger?"

In front of Brown sat Steven Yellity. The same thought was running through his mind, and he decided it was time to say something. Yellity's an interesting kid. He loves to read books by Jane Austen and Joseph Conrad and Nathaniel Hawthorne.

Also, he reads newspapers. Last summer, he read about Muhammad Ali supporting Ronald Reagan. And he's been reading about massive hunger throughout parts of the world and what he feels are inadequate efforts coming directly out of the White House to combat this hunger.

And it occurred to Yellity that Muhammad Ali should be in Washington, lobbying the wealthy and influential political contacts he made in the last election instead of asking donations from kids whose families, in a lot of cases, barely have enough food for themselves.

And yesterday he tried to say this in the auditorium at Douglass High.

He raised his hand, but nobody called on him. By this time, City Council President Clarence "Du" Burns was at the microphone, thanking Ali for coming to Baltimore.

Yellity kept his hand in the air, and now he began waving it back and forth. He felt foolish, felt as though everyone in the auditorium was watching him.

He's accustomed to feeling out of place. Though legally blind, Yellity's a voracious reader in a time when kids mainline television. He wears glasses that are like Coke bottles, and he's overweight, and there are insensitive kids who sometimes have fun at his expense.

And now, finally, Du Burns was calling on him, and Steven Yellity stood up and said, "Mr. Ali, is it true you campaigned for Ronald Reagan in the last election? And if so . . . "

"I can't answer that," said Du Burns, still standing at the microphone. "Mr. Ali, can you answer that?"

And Ali leaned into the microphone and said, "I'm not here to answer that question. We're here to talk about hunger, not politics."

"Why did you come to Douglass?" Yellity asked then. "Who else are you asking to help in this world hunger thing?"

And Muhammad Ali looked down at Steven Yellity, 5 feet 9 inches and 240 pounds, and said: "I can tell you ain't hungry, that's for sure."

The auditorium erupted in laughter. Yellity sat down, humiliated. But now his English teacher, Madeline Topkins, found the rage building in her, and so did Anthony Brown.

"Cheap shot, champ," Topkins shouted. "Cheap shot at a teenager. Steven can outthink, outwrite and outread anybody on that stage."

Jean Owens, principal at Douglass, rushed to the microphone and tried to be diplomatic, declaring, "This is not a political assembly. This has nothing to do with politics."

And Anthony Brown cried out, "Everything has to do with politics."

Last night, Madeline Topkins said, "The kids at this school do care about the needy. They've collected canned goods for hungry people. But no one up there was talking about the needy."

Anthony Brown said, "It was a promotional stunt, and they were playing on our intelligence. Why come to us? We're not wealthy people. We've barely got enough for ourselves."

And Steven Yellity said, "I'm the most disliked kid in the school now. I used to be Steven Yellity, nobody. Now I'm Steven Yellity, the person who assaulted Muhammad Ali. But I just thought it was unfair to make jokes while people are starving. That's all I wanted to talk about. And all he wanted to do was humiliate me."

But only for a moment, Steven.

Low blow, Muhammad Ali.

Winner on a TKO: Steven Yellity. He knocked the champ off his pedestal.

JANUARY 31, 1985

FACING DOWN THE ODDS

On the March morning Bobbie Collins found herself headed toward the delivery room at Mercy Medical Center, Bobbie's mother glanced at her watch and wistfully remarked, "Eight o'clock. I guess the kids are all headed for school now."

"Yeah," Bobbie said between labor contractions. "We have a big Spanish test today. I guess I can make it up when I get back."

She'd gone to school the previous day, completed her homework that night, and then she went into labor. The morning after she gave birth to a son, she had her parents bring books to the hospital so she could work on a term paper for English. She went back to class nine days after Damian Joseph was born.

She wasn't alone. On Friday, as the senior class at Southern High gathered at school for the last time, teachers estimated that about one-fourth of the girls in the graduating class already had children of their own.

There were no estimates on abortions, no figures on those who'd simply disappeared from school for reasons relating to maternity. There is now a program at Southern on parenting skills.

And last week an English teacher recalled, "A ninth-grader came to me one afternoon and said she wouldn't be in the next day. I asked why. She said she had to go for an abortion. She was 14. I told her I was sorry I asked."

On Friday, not only was Bobbie Collins among those gathered for a final morning at Southern, but her name was called again and again at a farewell awards assembly: as the school's top student in English, in mathematics, in science, in social studies, and as class valedictorian.

And now she sat in a little room, with classmates hugging goodbyes in a hallway outside, and Southern's principal, Cecilia Chesno, beamed proudly at Bobbie and mentioned her marks: a perfect 4.0 grade-point average, which translated to about 96 or 97 on a scale of 100.

"What'll you do in the fall?" Bobbie was asked.

"In the fall?" she repeated, running a hand through her blond hair, looking as though the thought hadn't occurred to her.

"Which college?"

"Well, nothing in the fall. In the spring, maybe I'll go to Villa Julie."

All plans are now reduced to maybes. She intends to marry her boyfriend in the spring, but he just started a new job, and he may be transferred out of town. So any college thoughts will have to wait for his employment possibilities.

"But I'll get to college," she said. "I'm not gonna be one of these women who sits at home with the baby. That would drive me crazy."

At Southern, roughly 40 percent of the graduates expect to head for college or trade school. There are about 150 in the class, although last Friday, at the close of school, it was not clear how many will qualify for graduation. When this class entered Southern four years ago, there were about 500 of them.

Where all the dropouts have gone, nobody can say. Of those graduating who now begin looking for jobs, no one knows the future. It's a grim employment season.

But the picture at Southern is vital, for the school is at once an oddity and an absolute microcosm of the city itself: odd, in that it's one of the last couple of city high schools with a truly integrated student body; but a microcosm, in that its 60:40 black / white student ratio mirrors the city itself, and thus offers clues about where we're heading.

"They're real nice kids," Principal Chesno says. "And this young lady is remarkable."

There's no question of that. But this city still has one of the highest rates of unwed teenage pregnancies in the country, and not everyone has Bobbie Collins's tenacity, or her brains, or her will to succeed.

Nor is Southern High alone in having roughly 350 of its original 500 kids from the class of '93 drop out somewhere between freshman year and graduation. And its junior class, which once had about 500 kids, is now down to about 180, with a year left to go.

On Friday, there were cheers in the school auditorium when the names of award winners were announced, and then everybody marched outside, teary eyed and filled with that mix of triumph and anxiety felt by all graduates.

They were lovely to watch. But the world doesn't greet them with open arms, and now some of their teachers stood there for a moment and took a last look at them.

"How many will find work?" one asked.

"How many of *them?*" said another. "Hey, I'm still looking for a summer job for myself, and I have no idea where that's coming from."

MAY 30, 1993

OVERCOMING THE FULL-COURT PRESS

Claude figures he's found an easy mark.

"A little one-on-one?" he asks, bouncing a basketball with his right hand and looking like Sergeant Bilko used to look when he'd innocently inquire, "Oh, is this game called poker?"

"You trying to hustle me?" I ask.

"Yup."

"You didn't get enough satisfaction the other night?"

"Nope," Claude says, and lofts a set shot from somewhere around the foul line.

Swish.

"Lucky."

"Wanta see it again?" Claude says.

You might say Claude's on a roll. He slides his wheelchair from left to right, bounces the basketball a few times, and launches another rainbow toward the hoop.

Swish.

"Lucky again," I tell him.

It's sarcasm as a zone-defense mechanism.

The other night, Claude and some of his buddies in wheelchairs taught a few of us some lessons about basketball and, not to make too much of it, about life.

Claude was born minus an arm and a leg, and he's got a little person's body from the waist down. He's 15 years old now and doing things neither God nor anybody on earth figured he'd ever do: He's on his way to leading a productive life.

The other night, we had a wheelchair basketball game at Children's Hospital's Bennett Institute. On Claude's team were kids who come to the gymnasium with him several times a week to build up bodies cheated by nature and by circumstance: kids with spina bifida, with cerebral palsy, kids who've had paralyzing accidents.

On my team were some media people blessed with good health and no discernible skills with either a basketball or a wheelchair.

The mathematical fact is this: Claude's team won, mine lost, and Claude is still rubbing it in.

What transcends the score is what happened on the court, a kind of fearlessness on the part of kids who once might have been written off.

In one moment, kids like Claude would drive the lane and plow through several wheelchair defenders to score. At the other end of the court, you'd find a basketball in your hands and immediately there would be defenders' hands in your face: kids who didn't see themselves as handicapped but merely as players in a ballgame, just like anybody else.

And once, there was maybe the most beautiful moment of the night. With the score tied late in the game, Claude drove for what looked like an easy score. It was a moment of personal triumph in the making.

But he spotted a teammate named Sammy, perched next to the basket. Sammy has spina bifida, a birth defect in which the spinal cord protrudes from the spinal column and damages the nervous system.

Claude passed up the easy score and tossed the ball into Sammy's lap. From the sidelines, where scores of parents had gathered, came cries of "Get it, Sammy."

And Sammy, arms fluttering, shot at a lowered basket. He missed.

Claude got the rebound. He gave it back to Sammy, who shot again. He missed. Claude got the rebound, handed it to Sammy, who shot a third time.

Swish.

The place erupted.

Each of us measures triumph and tragedy with different barometers. For parents along the sidelines, watching their kids play basketball goes beyond what they once might have dreamed. Bouncing a ball becomes cause for prayerful thanks. For the kids, it's a sweet taste of life that other youngsters take for granted.

"Most people look at these kids and ask, 'How do they keep going?' " Gwena Herman, coordinator of Physically Challenged Sports Recreation at the Bennett Institute, was saying after the game. "But these kids are like every other kid, and they've got the same desires and needs. Sports gives them something they can accomplish."

Like the other night, when Claude's team was merely wonderful.

"You want to try again?" Claude asks now, bouncing a ball casually. He arches another shot at the basket.

Swish.

This kid's got a lot of nerve calling himself handicapped.

MARCH 26, 1991

HOMELESS

In the 1700 block of North Broadway yesterday morning, somebody's furniture was piled on the sidewalk next to somebody's front door.

"Whose stuff is this?" you ask a couple of people sitting on cement steps a couple of doors away.

"The lady that used to live inside," says a woman in her late 20s.

"Yeah, that lady," the guy sitting with her agrees.

"Do you know her name?"

The two of them shrug their shoulders. They say the lady who used to live here had a little baby. The landlord wanted his rent. The lady who used to live here had no money to pay the rent, and the landlord came and put the lady's furniture on the street and locked the door when the lady wasn't looking.

"Any idea where she is now?" you ask.

"Somebody said she went to Chester Street," the woman on the step says.

"Family?"

"Bea Gaddy," says the woman.

A week ago, Bea Gaddy opened a place for homeless women and children in the 400 block of North Chester Street. There was much fanfare about this, with politicians venturing out of City Hall for about an hour, and reporters and photographers showing up and much TV coverage that night.

And now, only a week since the place opened, there are 16 women and 22 children inside, and word of mouth, which is stronger than newspapers or television, has already reached to the 1700 block of North Broadway, where this woman and her baby used to live.

On Chester Street yesterday morning, Bea Gaddy is standing in a tiny kitchen area, but only for a moment. She's telling a woman holding her baby in one arm how to rinse out a bottle properly. The woman is maybe 22 years old and looks as if she's hearing such instruction for the first time in her life. She says she last lived indoors at her sister's house, but that was several weeks ago.

A moment later, Gaddy is standing in an upstairs hallway while the shrill shrieks of another child split the morning air. Advancing on a corner room, Gaddy finds a child leaning out a second-floor window, while an infant sprawls on a bed and another toddler attempts to stick a baby bottle in the infant's mouth.

"Get that baby out of that window," Gaddy cries to the mother. Then, turning to the infant, Gaddy says, "What's the matter with this baby?"

"Baby's so spoiled, you can't do nothing with him," the mother says. She looks about 19.

"Well, who did it?" Gaddy says. It's more an accusation than an interrogation.

"Did what?" the young mother says.

"Spoiled the baby."

"Not me."

"Yes, you. Responsibility, young lady. That's what we're talking about." In the front room of Gaddy's place, there is a sign on a wall outlining rules for living at this center: You must get your education. You must get job training or seek employment.

This is a place for homeless women and children, which Bea Gaddy created in the wake of her own homelessness a few years back, but it's also a place to learn how to do better. When Bea Gaddy opened the place a week ago, she declared, "We're going to teach these women how to make it on their own."

The sound of her voice is a dare: I dare you to turn away from these people. I dare you to be heartless. Nobody thought she could pull this off, but she has. She did it by badgering people with money or influence or power, and shaming them, and refusing to let them turn their heads away from her.

But she faces an uncertain future: How do you keep money coming in faster than the conveyor belt bearing the city's homeless? She heads to the shelter's basement now. When it rained the other night, water from the alley behind the building swept into the basement, where spare furniture is kept. Gaddy looks around and steps carefully around this huge puddle of water.

"It's not the worst in the world," she says softly. "I've lived in worse."

Upstairs, the rooms are neat, the beds all made, the halls clean. The people who live here have come from all over town. Some of them found their furniture out on the street when they couldn't pay their rent. Others had no furniture, and no apartment, to begin with.

They're the lucky ones: They reached Bea Gaddy when she had rooms in which to put them.

"It's a sad world," Gaddy says, looking around a room filled with little children playing together. "It's a business that keeps you crying and praying and talking all the time. But I'm tired of crying."

She will go to the mailbox and she hopes there will be checks in the mail. And, if there aren't, she'll make phone calls to people with loose money. And if they're not in, she'll talk to people in downtown boardrooms.

And if none of that works—well, Bea Gaddy won't even imagine such a possibility. It's got to work. Because we can't keep letting women and babies wander the streets of the city with no place at all to call home.

AUGUST 1, 1992

THE BIO-UNDERCLASS

At the University of Maryland hospital yesterday, Wednesday, the third day of the brand new decade, there were 17 babies in the nursery. Wednesday's child is a child of woe: Seven of the 17 were born to drug-abusing mothers.

In the morning Dr. Hammond J. Dugan III, director of the full-term nursery, walked among the babies and wondered about the damage. Some of the babies are in active drug withdrawal, but some won't show symptoms until they've already gone home and the doctors and nurses can't reach them.

In either case, it isn't a pretty picture. The babies shiver and burn and move about fitfully. They can't coordinate their suck and swallow mechanism, and thus struggle to eat. They're sensitive to light and sound and have trouble sleeping. They cry more than other babies. Some will have brain damage. Some will have learning disorders. All will go home to families whose order has already been disrupted by drugs.

"I had a mother with a drug abuse problem in here the other day," Dr. Dugan was saying now, "and her child was going through withdrawal. It's her fourth baby. There's no husband, no male influence in the house. She lives on public assistance. And I said to her, 'What happens in the morning when you wake up and approach your day?' She said, 'I don't know. I just try to make it from one day to the next.' "

For most of these children, it won't be enough. In ever-greater numbers, the drug epidemic is now claiming not only the living, but those yet to leave the womb. What Charles Krauthammer called a bio-underclass is being created, a generation of physically damaged drug babies whose biological inferiority is stamped at birth like something out of Aldous Huxley's *Brave New World.*

At University Hospital, they estimate that maybe 15 percent of the newborn babies have mothers on drugs. At Johns Hopkins Hospital, estimates are similar. Some of these babies will get lucky and not inherit their mothers' narcotic dependencies, but many are in trouble from their first moment of life.

"It's clear," says Dr. Beryl Rosenstein, director of the newborn nursery at Hopkins, "that we're looking at an upward curve here. There's been a tremendous increase in mothers coming in with drug problems.

Four or five years ago, maybe 1 or 2 percent of the mothers were on drugs. Today, 10 or 15 percent."

That might be conservative. A year ago at University Hospital, Dr. Lindsay Alger and Dr. Marshall St. Amant did anonymous urine tests on 201 pregnant women and found 35 percent of them were doing cocaine, marijuana, or heroin.

Such women are notorious for not seeking prenatal care. But these women did. In other words, the rate was 35 percent among relatively responsible pregnant women.

But drug abuse figures are often a little fuzzy, particularly among babies. Some don't develop symptoms right away. If it's cocaine or heroin, there are usually symptoms in the first 72 to 96 hours. If it's methadone, the child might go three or four weeks without a symptom.

Now it gets tricky. The state of Maryland gives doctors only five days of observation. If treatment has begun by then, the state will pick up the tab. If it hasn't begun—and you don't treat a baby who hasn't shown symptoms—neither the state nor insurance companies will foot the bill.

Yesterday, of the seven babies at University Hospital born to drug-abusing mothers, several were in active withdrawal. One had been there for three weeks. Others were under observation, either because they were acting strangely or because the mother had given the hospital a history of drug abuse.

"A mother will say, 'I took cocaine 24 hours before my delivery,'" Dr. Dugan said. "She did it to get herself through labor. You know, we've got women delivering at home, opening themselves up with the drug. We've got kids in here who were born in the toilet."

Yet these doctors talk sympathetically about the mothers. Anger comes through, but mostly an understanding of the hopelessness of a lot of these women.

"You get angry and frustrated," says Dr. Rosenstein, "because you see what's been perpetrated on innocent victims. But you look at these women and you see they feel terribly guilty. They know this isn't right. But that's the nature of addiction. They can't control it any more."

And it's getting worse. It's the most poignant manifestation of the narcotics problem that doesn't go away, the problem that a generation of politicians has declared war against, only the war never quite kicked into gear.

And now, in the first days of the new decade, another generation is upon us, and they bring us the bad news not only about today, but about all of the tomorrows down the road.

JANUARY 4, 1990

BANDING TOGETHER; LETTING GO

The other day at Mergenthaler Vocational-Technical High School, Ronda Alston, 17 years old, stood on a stage between her classmates and all of their parents and commenced to sing like an angel.

The song came from *West Side Story*. The occasion was graduation day at Mervo. Ronda stood there with 357 classmates on the stage behind her, and an auditorium filled with parents in front of her, and now the words came out of her mouth:

> There's a place for us
> A time and place for us
> Peace and quiet and open air
> Wait for us
> Somewhere.

And you looked around the big auditorium, and you saw eyes glistening. The children on stage were about to be handed their adulthood papers. The adults sat there and remembered their own time on the edge of change.

Graduations do that for us. Most in the crowd were past 40 now, past the age when you've learned what not to hope for. Graduations let us remember not only a time, but a sense of anticipation and hopefulness that the world sometimes takes away.

And now Ronda Alston moved slowly across the stage, in front of the rows of her classmates beaming up at her, and she sang:

> There's a time for us
> Some day a time for us
> Hold my hand and we're
> halfway there
> Hold my hand and I'll take
> you there. . .

And a wonderful, spontaneous thing began to happen. In the front row, a boy reached out to take Ronda Alston's hand. And then a girl two seats down did the same. As she continued to sing, and to stroll across the stage, there were more hands reaching out from all the rows of Ronda's classmates, hands extending through the air to her, scores of them in the midst of this formal graduation ceremony, reaching for a hand to hold onto one last time.

It was beautiful to watch, and stirring, and maybe in that moment the kids at Mervo were all silently catching on: After this, they're on their own. High school is the last time you have a tribe to gather around you. There's no more sitting in class with the same gang. There's no more alphabetical order, where everybody knows his place simply by sitting behind the same person in each class day after day. Everyone has to go his own way in the real world, and you can't even copy answers off the kid in front of you any more, because everybody gets a different test from now on.

Then the clock begins to speed up. It takes 14 years to get through each single hour of math. After that, 14 years goes by in about an hour. In high school, everybody runs off in 18 different directions at once, mad to check out every horizon. After high school, you learn to pace yourself. You don't race breathlessly around every corner for something that maybe isn't there.

In *We Gave You the Electric Toothbrush*, Robert Thomas Allen wrote, "You don't grow old gradually, or on purpose, the way you go downtown on a subway. It's more like finding yourself standing in the last station wondering how you got there."

Adolescence is the last time you get to ad-lib your way through the day. High school is spring training for the rest of your life. Once the regular season starts, it's all business. Up in the morning, out on the job.

At Mervo the other day, there was Darnell Singleton. He was valedictorian and senior class president, and when he stood to speak the people in his class cheered him wildly. And Darnell threw back his head and laughed, and looked as happy as a national champion.

For most of these kids at Mervo, this is where formal education stops. Darnell Singleton swelled with pride when they announced he'd been hired by the Baltimore Gas & Electric Company for industrial economics. Other kids were cheered when they won awards for work in auto repair, in painting, in sheet-metal work.

That's where many of these kids will make their living now, and they won't hear the sound of crowds cheering them on.

In his final words to his classmates, Darnell leaned into the microphone and said, "I love you all and wish you good happiness and fortune always."

And you looked at this big, strong kid and felt he sensed something important. Big, strong kids are supposed to feel invulnerable. Kids graduating high school are supposed to feel indestructible. High school boys aren't supposed to be able to say "I love you." It exposes too much.

And yet Darnell said it, and his classmates cheered him madly. Nobody had to explain the future to them now. They were saying "I love you" not only to each other, but to the time they'd gone through together, as a tribe, a time they will never have again.

Then Ronda Alston sang like an angel to them, and they reached out to hold her hand.

Or maybe they were trying to put a hold on time itself.

JUNE 23, 1987

PLACES

Those in Need of Company Choose
the Throb of the City

The city renews itself when its inhabitants gather in public places. We remind ourselves at such moments that our neighbors are just like us, trying to scrape by in a difficult season. We rediscover that there are more things that unite us than divide us.

In the wake of the '68 riots, I thought the city began to be reborn with the first City Fair two years later. When the fair finally seemed to have outlived its charm, we turned to the Fells Point Festival and the Artscape festival. When we lost the Colts, we began lavishing previously untapped (and even unsuspected) love on the Orioles, who had always been a kind of afterthought to football.

Crowds make us realize we're not alone. Those who prefer solitude know they can flee to suburbia, but those in need of company choose the throb of the city.

When the City Fair opened, it made us realize how much we had invested in each other. When Memorial Stadium closed, it made us see how much history we had together: Men who first entered the ballpark as children, holding their fathers' hands, now entered one last time. And this time they were escorting their fathers. When such moments are right, they feel like the beating of a single heart.

ARTSCAPE: DANCING IN THE RAIN

This is what life in this city should be all about: Saturday afternoon at Mount Royal and Dolphin, with rain dripping out of a leaden sky and the radio telling everybody to stay home, people are dancing in the street.

It starts with maybe a dozen black kids at the Artscape festival, stepping lightly to music with a vaguely Caribbean beat. Within moments, a bunch of people have drifted out of the Mount Royal Tavern and the Maryland Institute and the food tents and the crafts booths and have ringed the dancers in a circle of scrutiny.

Now some of the spectators begin to join the kids. They are black and white and Asian. They slide several steps in each direction and punctuate the steps with hand claps. And still the numbers grow, dozens of people now moving to the middle of the street and ad-libbing their movements with the rain spilling on them and no one taking the slightest particular notice.

A man with an oil drum of a chest dances on make-believe Fred Astaire feet. He's next to a 10-year-old boy in a painted clown's face who's leaping into the air like a refugee from a Toyota commercial. Behind him is a woman with a silk skirt and an Orioles cap who's next to a toothless guy in Bermuda shorts and loafers with knee-high black socks who's alongside a pregnant woman dancing with her blond two-year-old son.

Now the rain picks up, and still more people join the dance. A woman wearing gold beaded sequins and high heels is swaying next to a guy dressed like Groucho Marx. He's dancing on roller skates. A few feet from him is a girl who looks like Tricia Nixon, dancing next to a fellow with a body like a praying mantis. And behind them all are two old folks, deaf to all melody, insensible to any beat and oblivious to everybody else around them, who are humming two different songs industriously and off key.

Forget the rain, the clothes that are sopping wet, the flirtations with every lurking pneumococcus. This is like a dance troupe composed of all of Western civilization. It's Holiday on Tar. While suburbanites huddle inside shopping malls and wait out the rain, the city of Baltimore says that Artscape, its annual artistic show-and-tell, shall go on.

In its way, the rain was the perfect metaphor for a city always struggling to find its way, asking surrounding neighbors to love it in spite of its storms, coaxing its own residents to dance with each other through the tough times.

Tough? A year ago, there were 71 thousand felonies committed in this city. In the district courts, where street crime comes to pay its dues, the caseload has gone up 55 percent in the last 15 years. In juvenile court, it's gone up 500 percent in the last 10 years. The cops estimate about 75 percent of all the crime is drug related.

And yet there is this: The city still spends more than $10 million a year on its cultural institutions, which figures out to about $14 per person. You want comparisons? It's seven times Baltimore County's rate, and ten times Howard County's.

Is there trouble in city schools? Don't ask. Funding for education in the city is $1,500 less per student than in Baltimore County. The drop-out rate's quadruple the county's, and the city's high school kids average 160 points lower on their college boards than kids around the state.

And yet there is this: The city employs 35 percent of the region's work force. More than half of all businesses and white-collar jobs are located in Baltimore. Nearly all of the region's major cultural institutions are inside the city's borders.

Is there money trouble? The city's assessable tax base has dropped by a third in the last 20 years. Half of all Marylanders living below the poverty level live in the city. About 60 percent of the city's babies are born out of wedlock, which generally translates to poverty being passed on as a kind of dismal legacy from one generation to the next.

And yet there is this: The city's various people have generally learned to live peacefully with each other. They bought William Donald Schaefer's hokum about Baltimore being best, and for the moment seem willing to be patient with Kurt Schmoke while he quietly patches things together.

For a long time, people stayed inside and played solitaire with their emotions. Summer street festivals were unthinkable. Walking anywhere downtown at night seemed a gesture toward suicide.

Now, with the economic numbers still stacked against it, the city no longer seems so afraid of itself. On Sunday, between the raindrops, there were clog dancers on a stage on Mount Royal Avenue, and half a block away two guys with their heads wrapped in towels played bongos. Nearby, a couple in pink and white silks danced on stilts that had ballet shoes at the bottom, and there was a long row of crafts just beyond the Meyerhoff Symphony Hall.

And the crowds kept coming and a light breeze took some of the edge off the killer humidity. The city's problems will not go away overnight. But sometimes, when people come out of their homes to celebrate their similarities as well as their bountiful differences, and they dance lightheartedly through the rain, you can look around and say: Yes, this is what life in this city is all about.

JULY 17, 1990

HERE'S TO THE FAIR

Chris Hartman would barge into the newsroom back then like a mudslide advancing on a small and helpless village. You wanted to run, but where? You wanted to stand up to him, but how do you confront a 300-pound editor who seemed to race in 16 different directions all at the same time?

"Gotta write this story," he said one summer afternoon 22 years ago. "This is gonna be the greatest thing in the history of this city."

Everybody thought he was crazy. The thing was to be called the Baltimore City Fair, and Hartman, then the assistant Sunday editor of the *News American,* had been brainstorming with all these people from the city's housing department, Bob Embry and Hope Quackenbush and Bob and Sandy Hillman and Dick Davis, and they were all talking about bringing the city back from the dead.

Can't be done, everybody else said. Too much tension downtown. Too much hangover from the riots two years earlier. Blacks and whites mixing in public? You'll have an atmosphere of fangs. Hartman, who majored in bluster, heard none of this.

"Here's who I want you to call," he said, grabbing any reporter not nimble enough to slip away. The energy was bursting out of his pores. P. T. Barnum, everybody in the newsroom called him. He was trying to put on a circus instead of putting out a newspaper.

But it turned out to be the greatest con job ever, and one that helped produce the salvation of the city.

The Baltimore City Fair was the emotional centerpiece of the thing we used to call the great renaissance. There's a certain sad shaking of the heads over that phrase now, owing to tough times, but this is mainly from people with no memory.

Two decades ago, this city's heart beat strictly by reflex. It was dead in its soul, frightened at the thought of strangers being involved in each other's lives. The big-money people were disdainful of investing in business districts or in neighborhoods. They hoarded their bucks and listened to suburbia's siren call. Those who lived here and had even a few dollars emotionally packed their bags and readied to move at the very next sign of trouble.

"The idea," Chris Hartman said that summer afternoon, "is to make the neighborhoods the center of this fair. It's a celebration of ourselves."

Everybody wished he would go away. Hartman could be overbearing and abrasive. Now he was just being foolish. Those others in the housing department, they were all such bright people, so plugged into the city's troubles, didn't they know any better?

All summer long, Hartman whirled through the newsroom: assigning stories here, directing coverage there, selling it hard. Boosting this bizarre idea, this City Fair. After a while, it wasn't just annoying, it was an imposition. You felt you should be covering real news, politics and crime and stuff, instead of the plans for this carnival.

And then, that September, as a city held its breath, something lovely happened. The fair opened its doors, and everybody in the world seemed to show up. Even nature helped, throwing in a minor hurricane that blew over neighborhood exhibits.

Instead of killing people's enthusiasm, it brought everybody together. Strangers began helping each other put their booths back in order and, in the process, found out this wonderful thing: They had more that bound them together than pulled them apart.

It went on this way for a long time, this Baltimore City Fair. It went on through very good years and then years when it began to feel like an afterthought, like an unwanted stepchild.

And then, the other day, they finally pulled the plug on the thing.

"Money," Chris Hartman declared. After all this time, he was on the fair's board of directors, still believing in the thing, still finding it a vital piece of the city's internal organs.

He needn't worry. They can call it quits on the fair, but it lives on anyway. Without the fair—without the clear signs it gave that people are hungry to get along with each other—this city would have dried up and blown away long ago.

Without the abundance of vitality it brought to downtown, there would be no Harborplace, no National Aquarium, no Maryland Science Center, no towering office buildings, and no expanded tax base, either.

For that matter, there'd also be no downtown ballpark, for who wants to enter an area where only shadows and ghosts wander about? Remember a team called the Baltimore Bullets? If only they'd stuck it out a little longer, they might have thrived here the way the Orioles are.

Without the fair's success, you'd have none of the ethnic festivals that followed, none of the neighborhood fairs, no Artscape. All these are spiritual children of the City Fair.

It did its job. After 21 years, its time was up. The idea was to revive downtown, and it succeeded beyond dreaming. The idea was to ease racial tension, and it did a lot of that, too.

And the idea was to make us believe in ourselves, and in our community, and that's the biggest thing the City Fair did. It deserves a rest. Remember it kindly.

JUNE 7, 1992

THE JOY OF URBAN LIVING

The three of us were trying to make a left onto Broadway when the old man marched up to the car, slapped one meaty hand on the hood, and shouted, "Your blinker's on."

"Thank you," I said. "It happens I'm making a left-hand turn."

"The left one," he announced to the immediate neighborhood.

"Yes, that's the one," I said. "I use it whenever I go left."

"Turn it off," he said. "It's blinking."

The guy right behind him had a body that looked as if some mad scientist had patched it together while nobody was looking. He was too big to be one of us. He wore a sweatshirt that said: "I am the person your parents warned you about."

From the back seat, the 20-year-old in my car took all of this in, inhaled deeply, and announced, "OK, I'm ready to go home."

She was never here before, poor thing. She's spent a life in the sterility of the surrounding counties, where people act alike. Her parents warned her about places like this, without ever actually venturing to a place like this.

"I heard it was dangerous down here," she said.

"It's not dangerous," said my daughter, who is her friend. Virtually since birth, my daughter has had this city thrust upon her. For a while, she complained it wasn't pretty enough. I assured her this was part of the city's charm. In her 19th year, the message seems to be getting through.

And so, on this glorious autumn afternoon, the three of us found ourselves walking through Fells Point, where thousands were gathering for the neighborhood's annual street festival to reassure ourselves that, even in a difficult time, the notion of a city renaissance still lives.

How do you explain Fells Point to a tourist from the distant outpost of Towson? Do you mention that it feels like the city's very own attic, with its cobblestones and its old bars and its old memories of immigrants landing here from distant shores? Do you point out that it looks like old black-and-white photos from generations ago, suddenly sprung to life?

Or do you just let Fells Point talk for itself?

On Thames Street, for instance, there were two teenage girls. One wore an earring that happened by dictate of fashion to be piercing her right nostril, and a bowling shirt. "I got an idea," she said. "Let's go get tattoos on our butts."

Her friend nodded her head as though this seemed a swell idea. The friend had prematurely green hair. The two of them were last seen weaving their way toward tattoo heaven.

Outside the Old World Antiques Co., on South Broadway, there was a vintage 1940s Victrola playing a 78-RPM record. It was "Red River Valley," by the Ranch Boys. It felt as if we'd stumbled across some lost artifact of a vanished civilization.

"I don't get it," my daughter's friend said, as people gathered to listen.

"There's nothing to get," I said. "It's just Fells Point doing what feels good at any given moment."

Across from the Cat's Eye Pub, in the middle of Thames Street, a fellow sat on a chair and played a guitar, a harmonica, and foot cymbals at the same time. He had a big guitar case in front of him, and there was a sign on the case: "Tipping is not a city in China." People tossed coins into the case, as much for the bad pun as for the music.

A few yards away stood a guy with tattoos running north and south on his arms and a vest opened to reveal the hairiest chest this side of Cro-Magnon man.

"What's it like to live in Fells Point?" somebody asked him.

"I don't know," he said. "I'm from Catonsville."

He just comes here to reinvent himself. Fells Point lets you do that. It allows you to be as anonymous as you like and therefore as unselfconscious as you like.

"This neighborhood?" said Mary Louise Preis, president of the Fells Point Preservation Society. "It's got the new, the old, and the strange. Where else are you going to find the president of Johns Hopkins University living next to a tugboat?"

She looks at the people all around her. "This neighborhood grew," she says, "because we didn't want roads here, we wanted people. And people have a tendency to adopt this neighborhood. You know, back in the '60s and '70s, we had young, rebellious people. A lot of them were angry. It was the times, I guess. But those same people still come here, only now they come around with their kids."

She says this as a woman walks past in a T-shirt that says: "Wild Women Don't Get the Blues."

Well, maybe. Thoreau wrote, "Cities are places where millions of people are lonely together." But sometimes, you get enough people together in a place like Fells Point, and it doesn't feel like loneliness at all. It feels like a tribal ritual, an affirmation of the value of urban living.

And maybe the 20-year-old in my car took a piece of that back with her to suburbia.

OCTOBER 10, 1989

CAN'T GO HOME AGAIN

The last baseball game at Memorial Stadium's been over for 40 minutes now, and most of the players are slipping away. They've sounded "Auld Lang Syne" on the public address system again and again, but 50,700 spectators just don't get the hint. The party's over, folks. Everyone go home.

Slight problem: Where do you go home, when this is the place you've called home for the past 38 years?

Let the record show that they played a major league baseball game at the 33rd Street ball yard yesterday, which they never will do again. And let it also show that almost nobody particularly noticed that Detroit scored seven times and Baltimore only once.

Forget the score. Game called on account of darkness.

When it was over, the boys of summers past took their old positions, scores of Orioles dating back to the spring of '54, as the theme from *Field of Dreams* sounded eerily through the chilly late afternoon haze. A dreamy kind of time-warp effect kicked in, and you knew that something was passing in front of your eyes for the last time. It wasn't a funeral exactly. But maybe it was your youth.

You could sense it in the ninth inning when, all through the big, darkening ballpark, a chant began to sound: "We want Flanagan, we want Flanagan." And then, as ordered, here was Mike Flanagan, the veteran left-hander, trudging in from the distance.

. It wasn't baseball at all; it was raw sentiment. Flanagan seemed to arrive not only from the bullpen but from some other time, from the late '70s and early '80s, from play-offs and World Series victories and that Cy Young Award that now seems like another world ago. As he struck out the last two Tigers hitters, his mere presence was a reminder: Oh, yeah, that's what it used to be like around here.

Give Orioles management some credit. They tried to bring off their move to Camden Yards with grace yesterday. They brought out some guys in white tuxedos who dug into the earth to pull out home plate. But the job took longer than expected. Home plate wasn't budging without a fight. And upstairs in Section 40, a guy's angry cry split the air: "Hell no, it won't go."

The sentiment was pretty general. When it was announced, "We'll take home plate to your new home at Oriole Park at Camden Yards," the crowd booed lustily. It was a reflex response, not so much a snub of the new ballpark as a sneer at the process that seemed to produce it: the flight of the Colts, the threat to move the Orioles, all the old ways changing against so many people's wishes.

It was a tough day for goodbyes.

"Don't call any errors today," a guy told official scorekeeper Bill Stetka before game time.

"How can I see errors when I'm crying?" Stetka asked, and then walked away.

"It's a heartache," a city cop named Donald Martin said early in the day. Out in pregame center field, the Baltimore Colts Marching Band suddenly struck up the first rousing notes of the old fight song.

"Chills," said Martin, turning his head. "It just gives you chills."

It was a baseball field spread before him, but you knew he looked out and saw the ghosts of Gino and Big Daddy, and Lenny and Artie, and Berry and Parker and the guy who wore No. 19. They won't be back this way again.

Later, as shadows began spreading across the diamond, almost like some curtain going down, an usher named Doug Hood stuck his head into the press box and asked if Al Kaline was around. If you have to ask the connection, you don't know baseball or you don't know Bawlamer. Kaline, the great Detroit outfielder-turned-baseball-broadcaster, was a kid out of South Baltimore. So was Doug Hood.

"I was Al's bat boy," Hood explained yesterday. "He played left field for Gordon's Stores. I saw him throw out a guy at home plate on the number 3 diamond at Herring Run Park. Al was on diamond number 2 when he did it."

Hood's never talked to Kaline in the ensuing 38 years, but yesterday he said, "Al's not here? Well, if you see him, tell him his old bat boy said hello. And tell him how proud he made us every time we saw him here."

You want pride? After they'd flown home plate down to South Baltimore, they started the eerie procession of old Orioles out to their former positions. Here came the music from *Field of Dreams*, and here came Brooks Robinson, loping out to third base.

If it didn't break your heart, then you have none to break. For 22 years, Brooksie's the one who brought summer to us, and now he was back, a little thicker through the middle, a little slower of gait. He seemed some ancient warrior, standing all alone for seconds that seemed like minutes.

And then came the other Robinson, Frank, jogging a little gimply out to right field. The first row of bleacherites all leaned over the railing, bowing like emissaries to a sultan. The heart thumped.

"I saw the first game here," 69-year-old Bernard F. Smith, in Section 40, declared. "I never thought I'd see the last."

A few seats away, a local social worker, Suzy Ricklen, 43, said, "There are enough things that change in the world. People come in and out of your life, but you figure buildings will stay."

In front of us, though, the people who had gone were now coming back en masse: Not only Brooks and Frank, but those from long ago, like Bob Boyd and Billy O'Dell and Chuck Diering and Bullet Bob Turley, who was there on that very first April 38 springs ago.

So we'd come full cycle. People filed out quietly as dusk settled. And you remembered back to the morning, as rain spilled out of a grimy sky and landed on Memorial Stadium. It seemed appropriate, actually. It seemed like an act of poetry committed by God, a final weeping over a dying ballpark.

OCTOBER 7, 1991

BLESSING AMERICA IN NORTHWEST BALTIMORE

Gerrie Highto ends the evening by accidentally moving the world.

"In honor of our boys coming home from the Persian Gulf," she says simply, "we want to sing 'God Bless America.' "

She's standing in this big room in Northwest Baltimore, at the Concord House residential center for the elderly, looking out at maybe two hundred people who have come to hear her Covenant Guild choral group perform.

The audience is beautiful. They're sitting there, many of them, in wheelchairs. Lots more have walkers and canes, and they're bundled in sweaters and housedresses. Some are around 90, and one lady has been playing an imaginary piano all evening in sync with the singers, who have been performing old Yiddish songs and Broadway tunes while much of the audience hums along and cheers warmly.

And now Gerrie Highto turns her back to the crowd, and she gives a signal to her 24 singers, and they begin to burst with the familiar words:

> God bless America
> Land that I love
> Stand beside her

> And guide her
> Through the night
> With the light
> From above . . .

At first she can't figure out what's happening. She notices one of her singers has tears coming out of her eyes. Then she sees another and another beginning to cry, and some are stifling sobs, and she thinks, "What is going on here?"

> From the mountains
> To the prairies
> To the oceans
> White with foam . . .

Now she begins noticing noises behind her, chairs scraping, the little tinkling of things moving about. And just as her singers get to the words "God bless America," she turns around and sees a little miracle happening in front of her eyes.

People are climbing out of their wheelchairs, and some are getting out of their seats by gripping their walkers, and they're holding onto each other as they clamber to their feet.

Now their ancient voices are rising in song, and a lot of the men are holding up their hands in salute. Many are clutching each other for support as they stand there. And behind her now, Gerrie Highto notices something new.

She can barely hear the voices of her own singers. Most of them are sobbing too loudly to get words out now, caught up not only in the sweet lyrics at this moment of the closing of the Middle East war, but at the sight of all these frail and elderly souls struggling to their feet to sing a song about their country.

And now the whole room is filled with voices singing, and with sobbing, too, and when it ends a few moments later the Covenant Guild singers start to rush out of the room. They want to compose themselves, they want to dry their eyes. But they can't get away. The audience is grabbing them, and they're hugging them, and they're kissing their hands.

"A magic carpet ride," Gerrie Highto says now. "We've sung 'God

Bless America' before. You always get reaction, but sometimes you wonder if some people think it's corny. But there's never been a reaction
like this."

Covenant Guild is a service and philanthropic organization of about
500 local Jewish women. They've raised money for the oncology department at Sinai Hospital and the Mount Washington Pediatric Hospital and the Kennedy Institute and for buses for the elderly. In all, they've
supported hundreds of charities. And any money they raise performing
goes to help these charities.

"But I've never seen anything like this," Highto says. "It came with
standing up and crawling up out of everything and tears and holding
onto each other. You know, most of the women in my singing group
are grandmothers, and they're standing there crying hysterically.

"The more people stood, the more they sobbed. And the singing is
coming out so meekly because the sobbing is so hysterical. And everybody is standing, even if they were holding onto somebody. It was a
sight to behold. Not just the elderly standing and saluting, but the
empty wheelchairs sitting around, and the empty walkers sitting there."

In the wake of victory in the Persian Gulf, everybody heaves a sigh
of relief. More than a decade after Vietnam, it's OK to feel good about
ourselves again.

MARCH 10, 1991

ABSENT FRIENDS

Life Is a Sprint

Growing up, we have the illusion that life goes on forever. Getting through a single hour of high school algebra can seem longer than the entire Bronze Age, so who could possibly imagine an end to life?

The older we get, the more we see life as a sprint and not a cross-country trot. The trick is to make the most of the brief run. What moves me about the people here isn't merely the dying, but the way they lived their time.

JERRY TURNER: WE LOVED HIM

The movie is called *Broadcast News,* and there's a reporter in it who tells his editor that serious television journalism is becoming an endangered species. It's a great, passionate scene. The reporter tells her how news is the important stuff, and not cosmetics, and he tells her how it's the story that's important and not the pretty faces with no brain cells behind them who deliver those stories.

And then, at the end of this long speech, the reporter looks at his lady boss and says, "And I love you."

The boss is stunned. The reporter shrugs self-consciously and says: "How do you like that? I buried the lead."

Jerry Turner would have loved the movie, and he'd have loved that scene. He was a working newsman who happened only by coincidence to be a celebrity. He came to work every afternoon and stayed until 11:30 at night, writing his own copy and editing other people's, and making sure nobody buried any leads, and he delivered the news with style and restraint and a gesture toward finding the best available version of the truth.

He knew all the surveys showed he was the highest-rated local anchorman in America, and more widely watched than anybody in the history of television in this town, and he was less impressed with himself than anybody you ever saw.

The secret of Jerry Turner's image? He insisted on seeing himself as an ordinary man, even when nobody else did. What you saw was what he was. Not a guy in an isolation booth, but your neighbor, who just happened to give you the news every night.

In Philadelphia yesterday, a fellow named Paul Gluck heard the terrible news about Jerry Turner's death, at 59, and let out a noise like a heart breaking.

Gluck used to produce the six o'clock news at Channel 13. Now he's at KYW-TV in Philly. Over the phone, he remembered: "He never had any sense of self-importance, the thing that distances celebrities from other human beings. He wasn't the pope moving through the masses, he was Jerry bopping through the crowd. That was Jerry. He bopped."

For the last year, he struggled. The cancer was eating at his insides, and yet he came to work between the various treatments, and even if you didn't know his life was ebbing, you saw a picture of grace under pressure.

And there are memories running through people's heads at Channel 13 now, snapshots of Jerry when he wasn't sitting in front of a television camera.

He went to the Burger King at Mondawmin Shopping Center one evening to pick up dinner for the 11 o'clock crew at the station. And this little kid walks through the crowd and looks up at him and says, "Are you the real Jerry Turner?"

"Yes, I am," said Jerry.

The kid says, "Look, are you gonna meet my mom and dad, or what?"

And, while everybody around him laughed out loud, Jerry said, "Sure," and marched happily through the crowd to meet the kid's parents.

"He was as natural as any broadcaster I've ever known," Al Sanders, Jerry's coanchor for the past decade, was saying last week. "When you watched him, you felt as if you really knew him. And you did. And I guess that's what he taught me—that as long as you're comfortable with who you are, you can be yourself on the air.

"I was his coworker, but also his friend. And I remember going to the ballpark with him one time, and there was no time to see the game. People were coming up every minute to shake his hand. And he was friendly to everyone. He was just Jerry."

Some of the things Jerry Turner did were unheard of for an anchor of his prestige. He spent his hours working, instead of selecting a wardrobe and combing his hair. He changed his own typewriter ribbons and got his hands dirty. It never occurred to him to ask for help. He had an office, but spent virtually all his time out in the newsroom with the troops.

And there was a handwritten sign that he used to hang from a wall in his office. It said, "There are two great tragedies in life. One is not getting what you want. The other is getting it."

He wasn't fooled by the trappings of celebrity.

Once, as he worked a story outside the old federal courthouse on Calvert Street, the traffic slowed to a near-standstill as drivers honked their horns and waved to get his attention.

Jerry shrugged and found it embarrassing.

Another time, during the explosive Roland Patterson era in city schools, Jerry covered a school board meeting where hundreds of people had gathered and were screaming angrily at each other.

Jerry walked in in the midst of it. Suddenly, everything came to a halt, and the crowd rose as one from their seats to give him a standing ovation. He apologized for intruding and asked everybody to please return to business.

He had a hair-trigger sense of humor, mostly about himself. In the days when Steve Martin was breaking in and wearing an arrow through his head, you could walk into the WJZ newsroom between broadcasts and see Jerry at his desk, writing copy, with an arrow through his own head.

Four years ago, when they started trying to make me into a television commentator, they explained I'd have to wear makeup in front of the hot, bleaching TV lights.

"Makeup?" I asked.

"Let's go," said Jerry, and he marched me into the men's room and took out his own makeup kit and began swabbing the stuff onto my face.

I was touched by this larger-than-life figure making such a big gesture. But he made nothing of it, which made it all the more touching.

And if you ever watched him on television, or if you knew him as a friend, you know one thing is true:

We loved him.

How do you like that, Jerry?

I buried the lead.

JANUARY 2, 1988

A NEW MEANING TO CONVERSATION

This is a kind of love story about two women who never even met each other. They were united by little messages scribbled and grunted across the years and by the disease that finally took them both.

The story's about people trying to hold on.

It's about JoAnn Churchill blinking her eyelids in a furious sort of homemade Morse code and people standing by her bed trying to translate, and it's about Shirley Sullivan slowly scrawling letters across a page through her own pain.

And it's about two people trapped inside their bodies and sharing a journey through illness that none around them, with all of their noblest intentions, could possibly understand.

JoAnn Churchill died the other day, 18 months after her friend Shirley Sullivan slipped away. They each lost out to amyotrophic lateral sclerosis (ALS), the muscular disorder also known as Lou Gehrig's disease.

"Remarkable women," the Reverend James Cronin, of St. Isaac Jogues Church on Harford Road, was saying yesterday. "Remarkable friendship."

He'd celebrated a memorial mass for JoAnn two weeks earlier. It was 41 years after he'd baptized her. It was six years ago, in one of a series of consolation visits to Shirley Sullivan, that he'd first told her of JoAnn and of their mutual affliction. "She's very ill," he told Shirley, "but she has happy days."

Shirley's were not so happy. She had a large family that gathered around her, but Lou Gehrig's disease is a relentless bully that neither love nor science has conquered.

"Shirley," Father Cronin said one day, "many people have health and physical comforts, but they don't have the love of a family like you have. You don't have health, and you won't have it. But if you had to choose between your family's love and your own health, which would you choose?"

She chose family, which became the foundation of her peace of mind.

And then came JoAnn. Father Cronin put the two women in touch, and it became a friendship that was part handwritten, part computerized, part simple hello across the emotional landscape.

JoAnn fought the disease for 12 years. For much of the last decade, she had to be fed through a tube and couldn't speak at all. She communicated by grunting, and when she no longer had the ability to grunt, she blinked her eyes.

"There was always someone with her," Father Cronin said. "Her husband Paul, her two sons, her parents, one of the nurses. I would come in and talk for a while. And when she wanted to give me a message, she would sort of moan. And this would clue the more informed person in the room to take over."

They'd run through the entire alphabet. When they'd reach the right letter, JoAnn would blink rapidly. It reminded Father Cronin of a kind of deathbed game of charades. With each run-through of the alphabet, a new letter was added until a word was formed. With each word, a sentence gradually took shape.

Always, Father Cronin was struck by JoAnn's frame of mind. "She rarely greeted you without a quick smile," he said. "Her acceptance of her misfortune was incredible and became a tremendous source of strength—not only to those who met her, but also to those who heard about her."

He figured JoAnn would be perfect for Shirley, who'd been struck by ALS in 1983. Shirley held on to small powers. She could scrawl letters across a page, slowly and painfully. She could speak, until the very end when her words became little more than a gasp.

She asked for JoAnn's address and began writing notes to her. They exchanged pictures. They lived within a few miles of each other but, over the course of six years, neither had the strength to visit the other.

JoAnn had her own means of communication—a computer, one of those miracles of modern science, onto which she could type a message by blinking her eyes. And, in this manner, she sent messages to Shirley—until she grew too weak even to work with the computer.

"So someone would run through the alphabet, and she would blink her eyes at the appropriate letter," Father Cronin said, "and very often she would be relating to Shirley, saying she'd gotten a card or a letter from her, or asking how Shirley was. And Shirley would tell me about getting a letter from JoAnn. And JoAnn's picture was always right by her bed. It was a beautiful, beautiful friendship they had, without either of them ever seeing the other."

The friendship ended 18 months ago, when Shirley died. JoAnn's family broke the news to her, and a day later, Father Cronin went to her house. When he talked to her of Shirley, he saw something that moved him deeply.

"It was about the only time I saw her cry," he said. "And her body literally vibrated with emotions, vibrated with sadness. She'd lost her kindred spirit. I don't know if she ever lost that sorrow."

The two women had such painful journeys. They had families that comforted them, and nurses and doctors to care for them, but they also had a disease that's relentless.

And so they turned to each other, making the most of scribbles and grunts and a furious blinking of the eyes that carried across the years.

MARCH 5, 1989

HORSEPLAYER'S FAREWELL

Everybody agrees Carl Schneider loved to play the horses, but nobody imagined how heavenly a horse would run for him a week ago.

Schneider, 70 years old, died last week of complications after a heart operation. He had a wife, Ida, and five children and five grandchildren and one great-grandchild, who were his love. And he had horse racing, which was his delight.

And this was why, on the day before Carl would be laid to rest last week, Ida Schneider asked one of her sons to drive over to Laurel Racetrack and get a racing form for the next day's races.

"A racing form?" the son asked.

"A farewell gesture," Ida said softly.

She knew, of course, of her husband's equine devotions. She knew he'd grown up in Bowie, not far from the track. She knew he'd always gone to the races at least once a week, sometimes with his son Earl, sometimes with his buddy Jim Dick. She knew that, win or lose, Carl would come home with a poker face and never tell how he'd done because either way, he'd gotten a day of fun out of it, which was the whole point.

And now last Thursday, on the morning after her husband would be buried, here was Ida Schneider reaching a hand into her husband's open casket and gently placing a Laurel racing form into the breast pocket of his suit coat.

From behind the casket now came the Reverend Ed Droxler, of St. Joseph's Church in Odenton. As he began his eulogy, Father Droxler happened to glance down at the casket.

Now his head began to spin a little. Father Droxler has been a priest for 44 years, and he's seen many items placed in coffins next to the dearly departed. Never, in all those years, had a racing form been among them.

And now the good father's mind did a slight backflip, to that morning's six o'clock mass at St. Joseph's. At the end of services, he'd heard two parishioners talking. He knew they were horse players. He remembered one of them that morning saying to the other, "Millersville. Fourth race at Laurel. Gotta get some money to put on him."

Father Droxler has a philosophy about funeral services. He does not like to belabor the tragic. He wishes to lift people's hearts with the amusing anecdote, the glad memory, the suggestion of a life well spent.

He had one personal memory of racetracks, of years ago, when a friend took him to Aqueduct, handed him $50, and said, "Enjoy yourself."

For two races that day, Father Droxler merely watched the horses run. As the third race loomed, however, he noticed a horse would be running with a lovely name: Lord's Angel. Father Droxler said to himself, "Let me take a chance," and put $2 on what seemed to be a heaven-sent message.

Lord's Angel won and paid $80.

And now, at Hardesty's Funeral Home in Gambrills, the good father looked down again at the racing form in Carl Schneider's coat pocket. Fourth race at Laurel, he thought. Millersville, he thought. As he looked across the rows of mourners who'd come to say farewell to Schneider, Father Droxler began to talk about the things running through his head. "You know," he told the mourners, "I don't know how the horses are running up in heaven. That's not my thing to say. And I didn't know Carl, but I understand by seeing the racing form that he was a fan."

A ripple of acknowledgment swept across the mourners.

"As it happens," said Father Droxler, "I have a hot tip on a horse which someone gave me. Called Millersville, at Laurel, the fourth race today. Wouldn't it be funny if we put a little bet on that horse and it came in?"

The ripple of acknowledgment became a soft wave of laughter which lingered. Later that afternoon, after Carl Schneider had been laid to rest, his family went back to his home to sit for a while with his widow.

"Wouldn't it be funny," somebody said, "if we put a bet on that horse the father mentioned?"

"Yeah," somebody else said, "wouldn't it be funny?"

And, just like that, people started opening their wallets and somebody was putting all the money into a little pile until it reached about $60.

That afternoon, a couple of the men went over to Laurel. They saw that Millersville was a long shot. They saw that a horse named Home Run Harry was the favorite. They saw that another horse, named Eternal Charmer, was considered a pretty good bet.

But they had romance in their souls, and $60 in their pockets which they put on Millersville.

Millersville led wire to wire—and paid $14.20.

Father Droxler heard the news the next morning. Somebody telephoned to say that the horse had won, and his little funeral tip had been worth about $400.

What he also heard was the thing that happened after the men got back to Carl Schneider's house from the racetrack.

They handed Ida Schneider the $400.

It was for Carl Schneider's last great day at the track.

OCTOBER 4, 1990

A FULL LIFE, NOT AN APOLOGY

Favorite snapshot of Charlie Cherubin: Twenty years ago outside City College the cops have arrested him for the crime of behaving like a citizen.

Charlie loved that picture. It ran on the front page of the *Sun,* and then the wire services picked it up, and Charlie's brother Lester saw it in New York and called long distance to tell him he'd seen it in the *New York Times.*

Naturally, the cops had to arrest Charlie. It was 1967, and they were arresting teachers all over town. The teachers were striking. The cops arrested them for the crime of peacefully walking picket lines outside of schools.

"Sam Banks and I were the first ones arrested," Jerry Levin was remembering yesterday, two days after Charlie Cherubin died. "And then Charlie was arrested. It was right outside City College. And the kids from City came down, and they saw what was happening, and they were going to turn the police car over. We had to talk them out of it."

Favorite high school memory of Charlie Cherubin: He was adviser to the City College newspaper, the *Collegian,* back in the days when the paper came out every single week of the school year. And there was no high school paper in the country to compare to it. That's not just an old alum talking. In those days, Columbia University used to rate all the high school papers every year, and the *Collegian* was judged the nation's finest.

But not so you'd hear it from Cherubin. He'd march into the little *Collegian* office, where he used to sneak cigarettes between English classes, and he'd sit all of us down. City was an all-male school in those days. And, in that sandpaper voice of his, he declared one day: "You're not working hard enough. The paper isn't good enough. You all want to get into good colleges? You want my recommendation? Well, I have letters of recommendation in my desk drawer that could get you into a convent."

Favorite hospital story of Charlie Cherubin: Several days ago, when things were looking bad, when he'd lost 50 pounds and the cancer was wasting him and he could barely speak, a nurse at Hopkins Hospital put him on a gurney and wheeled him down a hall.

In the last moments of his life, Charlie struggled to a sitting position.

"Lay down," said the nurse.

"Lie," said Charlie.

"What?" said the nurse.

"Lie. Lie down," said Charlie, the old English teacher correcting wayward verbs to the last.

He was the one behind the 29 rules of grammar all City students had to memorize. He used to say, "It's important to know grammar. It distinguishes you from the engineers at Poly, who can barely write their names."

It's funny to find out, so many years later, that he was the one behind all those grammar rules. You think of strict grammarians, you imagine uptight personalities. Charlie Cherubin was the freest of spirits, a 69–year-old flower child, a man who knew literature and art, who was a chef, a painter, a mechanic, a gardener, a man whose mind and soul were always open for business. He grew up in an orphanage, the Hebrew National Orphan's Home, in New York. His father left home when Charlie was seven, and he and his brother Stanley were sent to the orphanage for the next 10 years while his mother raised the two younger children.

A few weeks ago, somebody found an old friend from the orphanage, a guy named Manny Bergman. The last time he'd seen Charlie was 1934. Bergman called Charlie's hospital room while Charlie's daughter Jan sat next to his bed.

"This is Manny Bergman," said Manny.

"Manny Bergman," Charlie said. "It's 1933, there's a snowstorm at four A.M. The night watchman wakes me to hitch the horses to the snow plow. I go downstairs and look across a field and see Manny Bergman on the ground, working on a car. You were up before me."

When he got off the phone a few moments later, he turned to his daughter. "See what I did?" he said. "I gave that guy a memory. Instead of b.s.ing about my health, I gave him a memory."

He was still giving his children lessons in his final days. The lesson he gave everybody who knew him was to live a life and not an apology.

"You have to do the right thing," he told his daughters, Jan and Rachel. "Don't worry what the other person's doing."

Jan sat up all night with him recently. She remembers his asking, in a kind of hallucinatory tone: "Is this a play?"

"I wish it were," she said.

"Well, what is it?"

"It's a life," she said softly.

"Do we have to act it out?" Charlie asked.

And yet, in every other way, he wanted to act out life to its fullest, and he did it with wit and energy and an edgy curiosity, and a kind of intellectual fearlessness.

And that's not a bad epitaph for any schoolteacher.

FEBRUARY 19, 1987

THE END OF A RADIO ERA

Eddie Fenton was the greatest one-eyed, gimpy-legged, hard-drinking, tough-talking radio reporter who never drove a car and never took a note and never missed a deadline eight times a day.

He spent four decades filing stories every hour at WCBM radio and he knew 47 different ways to beat you on a story, including stealing your duplicate copy and reading it over the air before you could get it into print. Was he legendary? He covered so many demonstrations, it was said the city cops didn't send out the Tactical Squad until Eddie showed up.

Was he reactionary? One day, former Governor Blair Lee walked away from Eddie shaking his head in disbelief. "He's angry with me," said Lee, "because I refuse to appoint Idi Amin to the parole board."

Was he pugnacious? At a City Hall press conference commemorating Girl Scout Week some years back, Eddie brusquely asked William Donald Schaefer, "Mr. Mayor, is it true that your mother is the prime contractor for the Aquarium?"

"Eddie," the mayor shot back, "you're the only man I know who's suggested we build a distillery at the Aquarium."

At the courthouse, and at City Hall, and in the State House in Annapolis, the people who worked with him and those he covered were all remembering Eddie Fenton stories this week, after Fenton, 70 years old, died last Friday night.

Was he a fair reporter? Though Eddie had strong political convictions, he never let them creep into his stories. Once, he even reported something negative about his friend Mimi DiPietro, the city councilman who let Eddie stock his booze in Mimi's City Hall refrigerator. When Mimi heard he'd been slammed on the air, he confronted Eddie and uttered the immortal words, "Fenton, you're trying to scruple me."

Was he inventive? When Eddie covered criminal cases, he'd find a telephone booth with sightlines to the courtroom. With the jury still emerging from deliberation and every other reporter still sitting in court, Eddie would already be on the telephone with his station, sending in the story.

How did he know the verdict? He'd have Roland Baker, the senior criminal courtroom clerk, give him signals: one finger for a guilty verdict, two for innocent. "Except," Baker explained yesterday, "Eddie's eyes were so bad, I had to stand out in the hallway and hold up one whole arm for guilty, and two for innocent," as though signaling a touchdown.

Was he irrepressible? Radio newsman Ron Matz remembers his first City Hall press conference, when Mayor Tommy D'Alesandro mistakenly thought he was running City Hall. "It's this big ceremonial room, and Eddie's on pins and needles because it's getting near his deadline. And the mayor walks into the room, and Eddie grabs the phone right behind the mayor's desk in front of all these reporters, and he calls his station with one hand and, with the other, he grabs the mayor and interviews him live while everybody else sits there watching."

It was Matz who used to give Eddie rides everywhere. As a teenager, Eddie admitted once, "I figured I had two choices: You drink or you drive a car." Thus it was that Eddie's colleagues knew him as the one-man carpool with the X-rated vocabulary.

Was he abrasive? The day Westinghouse Broadcasting's Val Hymes first walked into the State House press room, Eddie declared: "A broad? Now we can have someone wash out the coffee cups." Hymes later named him Male Chauvinist of the Decade.

Was he profane? As dean of the Annapolis press corps, it was Eddie's job to signal the end of Marvin Mandel's news conferences by saying, "Thank you, governor." When another reporter had the nerve to utter the words, Eddie surged to his feet and bellowed across the room, "You ever do that again, and I'll break your ——— neck."

Then he turned to Mandel and said, "Thank you, governor."

"Thank you, Eddie," said Mandel.

Was he creative? When George Wallace was shot, Eddie went to Laurel and needed an edge. He spotted an old man outside his house looking at the crowd. He walked up to the old man and told him, "I'll give you $10 if I can have exclusive use of your phone."

Later, the old man was turning down $100 offers from other reporters desperate for a way to reach their editors.

Did he have a sense of perspective? Once, Eddie called WCBM from Annapolis. Richard Sher, then assistant news director, answered the phone.

"Put me on the air," said Fenton.

"We're still one minute away from the news," said Sher.

"Break me in right now," demanded Fenton. "Tell 'em it's a bulletin."

In an instant, Sher was announcing, "Let's switch to Annapolis for this bulletin." And then came Fenton, declaring triumphantly: "The beer tax is dead! The beer tax is dead! This is Eddie Fenton, for WCBM News."

Is this the end of an era in Baltimore radio? You figure it out. Eddie ended his four-decade career at WCBM in 1980. On Saturday, when a reporter called the radio station for a reaction to his death, nobody there had ever heard of him. "Well," the reporter mentioned, "you might want to mention his death on the air."

"Nah," he was told, "we don't do local news on weekends."

NOVEMBER 3, 1987

ALAN "THE HORSE" AMECHE

The newspapers say that Alan Ameche, The Horse of Baltimore Colts football, had a heart attack and died the other day, but the newspapers have it slightly wrong.

No one dies if we remember him. To a generation that made the Colts a religion, and adopted the players as members of an extended family, Ameche remains indelible.

He didn't die. He just joined the alumni association of the living.

Always, in the places we keep our memories, it will be twilight at Yankee Stadium. Always, Lenny Moore and Jim Mutscheller and George Preas have opened a hole wider than the New York subway system. Always, here comes The Horse, hurtling into the end zone, forever in his youth.

The newspapers make much of that touchdown, and yet they miss some of its importance. Yes, it gave the Baltimore Colts that 23-17 sudden-death championship win over the New York Giants. Yes, it electrified a nation that once considered professional football an after-thought to the college game.

But it was more than that.

It lifted a city out of its long municipal inferiority complex. It took a community that existed in a kind of stepchild culture, the gawky kid nestled on a railroad line between New York and Washington, the working-class town buried between two glittery media centers.

If you were alive in Baltimore that day, the feeling has never gone away.

If you went to the old Friendship Airport that night, when the Colts' plane taxied in from New York, you saw 30 thousand of your neighbors in a state of pandemonium.

"They're all drunk," said one panicked Colt.

"No, they're not," said a sportswriter who'd grown up here. "They've just waited all their lives for this."

The newspapers say pro football is just a business now, but some remember a time when it was a passion. Alan Ameche's death reminds us of such a time. The newspapers say the players are only in this for the money now, but in Ameche's time, there wasn't much money, only the love of the game, and people in the stands living at the top of their emotions.

For Ameche, it will always be December of '58. Or maybe September of '55, when a quarterback named George Shaw handed him the football for the first time as a Colt, and Ameche rumbled 79 yards with it. The previous year, the Colts had won three games. In a single play with Ameche, they were suddenly a force.

The mind is a camera with a recording device. The sound of advertising jingles recalls not only a time, but a state of mind. In this town, in that Colts era, everybody'd go to Gino's, if they didn't meetcha at Ameche's.

Ameche and Gino Marchetti put together one of the most successful hamburger operations in the country. In those days, if you attached the name of a Colt to a business, it seemed to take off automatically. In his time as a Colt, Ameche never made more than $35,000 in a season. As a businessman, he made millions.

And yet, there's a scene that's indelible. A couple of years ago, on York Road, I'm sitting with Art Donovan. He's waiting for Ameche, whom he hasn't seen in a year. And now Ameche comes into the room, and here are the two buffaloes, in their 50s, bounding across the room and enveloping each other in hugs.

This is not the way businessmen greet each other. Football games are only a business to people who've forgotten the way things felt.

The newspapers say Alan Ameche wasn't an emotional guy, that he didn't dwell on that sudden-death touchdown that won the championship. On York Road that day, though, Artie Donovan remembered a different Ameche. He remembered a time in 1978, when CBS-TV gathered the Colts and the Giants together for a touch football TV replay of the title game.

"The night before the game," Donovan remembered, "some of us got together in a bar, and they showed us a tape of the '58 game. Here's John Unitas, studying that film like he was taking notes in his playbook.

Everybody else is hooting and hollering, and John's still the professional.

"And then comes the overtime, and I'm sitting next to Ameche. And we're all watching, and it's quieter now. And, as Ameche goes into the end zone, Ameche on the bar stool covers his eyes, and he begins to cry."

In his autobiography, *Fatso,* Donovan remembers another time of sadness, a few years ago, when Ameche's son was killed in a car crash. "A lot of Alan's former teammates from Baltimore went up," Donovan remembered. "We went to his house for the wake. And I have never witnessed anything as sad in my life. . . . I'll never erase the memory of The Horse and his wife and the rest of the kids standing around that little boy in the coffin. After the ceremony, Gino and I were standing out on the veranda, and the next thing anyone knew, war stories about the Baltimore Colts were gushing. And I spotted Alan, a sad smile creasing his lips as he listened. As we were leaving, one of Alan's sons came up to me and said, 'Mr. Donovan, that's the best thing that could have happened to my father. You let him know he has people in the world who love him.'"

That's what the newspapers are trying to tell us now. But the newspapers write the facts and sometimes miss the emotions of a time and a place. It's 1988, but a man's death takes us all back 30 years.

Alan Ameche's kind of lucky. He was 55 when he died, but he gets to remain 25 forever in people's hearts.

AUGUST 11, 1988

A BIG KID WHO HAD HELP FROM THE ANGELS

Mr. Diz went through life with his inhibitions down and his volume turned all the way up.

He looked as though he'd been invented inside Damon Runyon's head on a particularly fertile day and dressed in the dark on a very bad morning. He'd wear a heavy overcoat, followed by a sports coat, a sweater, another sweater, a shirt, and maybe another sweater to boot, and wear them all whether he was sitting in a courtroom or hustling balloons at a parade or unsuccessfully hollering a long-shot home at the Pimlico finish line.

The first time I saw him, he walked into John Steadman's old sports office at the *News American* and started recreating Clem McCarthy's broadcast of a Kentucky Derby finish of maybe 30 years earlier. Arms waving, voice bellowing, spittle flying, by the time he finished, the entire third-floor editorial department had gathered and was cheering as though they'd all spent their rent money on long-shot bets.

This was 19 years ago, when Mr. Diz was 47. He looked ancient even then, harried and haggard and out of breath. But he had the glad heart of a child until it gave out on him last week, at age 66.

The angels kept Mr. Diz alive for the longest time. That's what he called them, his angels. They were the guys who'd bankroll him for a week's rent or a day at the races, some of which were triumphant and most of which were disasters.

He claimed he'd won $40,000 one day at Garden State Park, but gave it back to the horses in six months. He lost $5,000 in a single day at the same track, when a horse named Turbine was beaten in a photo finish and Diz literally broke out in a rash waiting for the call.

But the angels kept coming through for him. He was always in debt, and always calling on his angels. One time he made a little list of the people he owed money. The list was 82 pages long. "Isn't that amazing," he said thoughtfully, "that a guy who doesn't have a job can owe so much money to so many people?"

He said the tab came to $96,232.43. Of course, that was years ago. There's no telling where it was at the end, but if Diz was keeping score, it's unlikely any of the angels were.

Most of them saw him for what he was: an innocent at heart, a man with his defenses down, a big kid who simply couldn't settle down.

He tried giving up the track some years back, and started hanging out in courtrooms. It was a natural. He'd known judges and attorneys for years, from taking bets to the track for them.

But the racetracks were his home. In fact, for years he lived in an apartment just off the three-quarter pole at Pimlico.

The closest Diz came to steady employment was serving with the U.S. Army. At Anzio, where he was an ammunition carrier with an infantry outfit, there were enemy shells flying when Diz organized a race with donkeys and called it the Anzio Beach Derby.

He'd gotten the racing bug early. A seventh-grade dropout, he followed a carnival troupe south, peddling balloons and cotton candy and

Brazilian bubble gum, and at age 14 found himself in Miami, where he discovered a magical place called Hialeah Park.

He'd hang around, parking cars and hawking newspapers, and now and then whisper a tip to a customer. Sometimes the tips paid off, and the customers thanked him with money. This is known as breaking the law. Miami police invited him to leave the state of Florida.

As usual, though, Diz was broke. He called a friend in Baltimore for money, and the friend sent it to him. Diz immediately blew it at the track and had to hop freight cars all the way back home.

He was uninhibited, but far from insensitive. Loud and full of laughter in public, he called himself a lonely man who went home alone at night. He said he'd "caught arthritis" selling balloons in the rain one year and wore a copper bracelet to try to fight it. He carried two chestnuts in his pants pockets, which he said cured him of leg pains.

He said doctors wanted to give him butazolidin, but Diz balked. Bute was the stuff they gave racehorses, but the horses weren't allowed to run on it. If it wasn't good enough for them, it wasn't good enough for Mr. Diz.

Pimlico owner Ben Cohen named a few horses after him—the aptly named Mr. Diz, and the even more aptly named Always Broke—but Diz never made any money off either namesake. Mr. Diz (the horse) won a lot of money, but Mr. Diz (the man) either didn't have money to bet on him or was afraid to, lest he bring it bad luck. Always Broke always was, and was sold.

It was Steadman who gave the formal nickname to Diz. His real name was Frank Rosenfeld (a name he never wanted to see in the newspaper, so creditors couldn't track him down), but after suffering dizzy spells during the war, some guys called him Dizzy.

Steadman added the Mr. because he felt everybody deserves a little dignity.

MARCH 3, 1985

JAZZ TO SOME, SUBS TO THE REST

Harley Brinsfield talked in equal parts jazz shorthand, Eastern Shore slang, and the sentence fragments of a man in too big a hurry to stay on a straight linguistic path.

When he talked on the radio six nights a week for a quarter-century, he was a missionary of half-remembered music for a couple of generations of Baltimore listeners. In his cynical moments, he said he only played music to hustle his famous Harley sandwiches. He was lying. He only sold sandwiches so he could play music on the radio.

Jazz was Harley's hard-core addiction, and the people who played it were his benevolent suppliers. Some of them stayed with him when they came to town. Many were black and couldn't get hotel lodging in preintegrated America. Harley took them in. "There were one or two places they could go," Harley recalled one afternoon years later, "but they were afraid of going up there and being embarrassed. So they'd come and stay with me."

He took in Louis Armstrong and went with him to a shoe store on Pennsylvania Avenue on Christmas around 1950. Armstrong was playing the old Royal Theatre then. He had $1,000 on him, Harley said, and he bought shoes for every kid lucky enough to walk past.

He took in Billie Holiday when the dope dealers were gravitating to her. In his McMechen Street apartment, he'd sit up half the night as the great singer reminisced about her youth in Baltimore and struggled without luck to stay off the hard stuff.

When he went to New York's Metropol one time to hear the great Red Allen's band, he invited all the musicians back to his hotel afterward for deli and imported beer. But the hotel management wouldn't let the band come in, for reasons owing to skin color. So Harley grabbed the food and drink and went to the musicians' hotel.

It was the son, Harley Jr., who remembered the last story yesterday, when he called to say his father had died, at age 81.

It was Red Allen who'd told Harley about Billie Holiday nearing the end. She'd taken a drug overdose while working a club in Chicago. Allen needed a fill-in. He grabbed a wardrobe girl named Ruth Jones who sang a little, put her in an evening gown, and made up a name to introduce her to the crowd. He called her Dinah Washington.

Human beings leave behind not only the central core of their lives, but the little sidebar stories that go with them. With Harley's death goes a name synonymous with jazz, and with the submarine sandwiches he sold at dozens of places around town. To many Baltimoreans, the Harleyburger and the Harley's Original were as much a part of the culinary landscape as steamed crabs or nickle coddies or snowballs on hot summer nights.

For a couple of decades, Harley's nightly jazz show was carried over local radio. If you listen closely, you can still hear the echo of the opening and closing, with Clancey Hayes singing, "Come on, Nancy, put your best dress on / Come on, Nancy, 'fore the steamboat's gone . . . "

One night in the '50s, his station carried news reports of a murderer's execution at the state penitentiary. The execution ran late, while Harley fretted back in the studio and wondered if his audience would stick around.

Finally, a reporter named Charlie Roeder declared, "The lights are now lowering at the penitentiary." The condemned man having been dispatched to his creator, an engineer signaled to Harley that he was on the air. His opening words: "Well," Harley drawled, "I know one cat who ain't gonna be diggin' the show tonight."

Harley's love affair with the music started when he was a kid in the Eastern Shore town of Eldorado and ran off to hear the spirituals of the itinerant factory workers and farm laborers and the jazz that wafted out of the local pool hall.

At 13, he'd run off to the Black Cat Inn, outside Wilmington, to hear the greats like Fletcher Henderson's old band. Harley stood outside the windows of the inn, and the black musicians would see his face at the glass. "There was such rapport between us," Harley remembered, that when they'd finished their set, the musicians would gather a kitty of a buck or two to get him back to Eldorado.

"I feel like I'm doing a service in initiating people," he said one time about his radio show. "They don't really know how great jazz is. It's just a thing to them until it strikes their central intelligence system."

If you were lucky enough to be invited to Harley's apartment, where many of his 20 thousand recordings were kept, you'd feel as if you were stepping into history. He'd known Duke Ellington and Dave Brubeck and Eubie Blake and the old rocking chair lady, Mildred Bailey.

"She told me once," Harley recalled, "that she needed cancer treatments every year for 15 years. She'd go to the Mayo Clinic. And every time she went to pay the check, they'd say, 'We won't take it, we're doing it for science.' But she told me, the last time she was there, she found a fellow who'd been paying her bills. Just because she'd gotten him a job years earlier. His name was Bing Crosby."

That's the kind of stuff Harley Brinsfield carried inside of him, and it's the stuff he'd tell his listeners over the radio.

If they've got a microphone up in heaven, somebody ought to be hustling a lot of hot Harleyburgers and cool jazz over the radio tonight.

MAY 8, 1990

THE BEAUTY OF THE *PRIDE*

In a dim restaurant in Fells Point, she rummages through a pocketbook. Outside, tugboats nestle gently at the foot of Broadway. A notebook is in her pocketbook somewhere, and she wants to read some lines that she found in a book and copied down.

The newspapers are filled with death today. Nature has overwhelmed the *Pride of Baltimore,* and two people are dead and two more still missing somewhere in the vast Atlantic.

She can't remember where she discovered the lines, but she finds the notebook and begins to read, and to connect the words to people from the lost ship. But, more closely, to the rest of us:

> Though the physicality of death
> Destroys the individual
> The idea of death can save him.
> Contemplate death if
> You would learn how to live.
> By keeping death in mind
> It passes into a state
> Of gratitude, of appreciation
> For the countless givens of existence.

We mourn the death of the *Pride of Baltimore* as we never appreciated her in life.

Actually, that's an understatement: In life, the *Pride* captured very few hearts. A lot of people saw her as frivolous, an expensive, in-group plaything for political and corporate heavyweights whose social lives revolve around Harborplace while whole sections of the city struggle for daylight.

The *Pride* seemed a party that only a select few ever got to attend. If we saw her at all, she was sailing across our TV screens on the evening news. The people behind the *Pride* thought this made the ship important and beloved: "Look, there she is on the news! Doesn't that say something about people's love for her?"

Absolutely not. The *Pride's* value to the TV people was strictly her photogenic quality: She was lovely to look at, gliding across a sunset. But she failed to connect emotionally beyond that.

And many people resented her, or were only dimly aware of her, for being no more than a pretty plaything of the rich. The people behind the *Pride* took umbrage at this, and attempted to justify her existence. They talked of the *Pride* sailing off to foreign ports as a goodwill ambassador hoping to attract lots of overseas interest, and money, to Baltimore.

They got it all wrong. They defended her on financial grounds, instead of selling us on the truth: Her crew led the kind of lives that are lost to the rest of us. Most of us on land go through life as though it's a practice run for something better yet to come. We make our lives out of not living, out of being spectators at other people's lives. And we put off those primal urges inside, the wild, half-buried desire to rush off, tell the boss to go to hell, shout to friends, "Gotta go. It's late, and the rest of my life has been waiting up for me, sitting outside my window and hoping I'd show up so we can feel our pulse beating for a little while."

At the restaurant in Fells Point, we talked about life passing us by. Those people on the *Pride of Baltimore* wouldn't understand what we were talking about. Life hadn't passed them by, because they'd attacked it on its own terms, and no one else's. They'd decided what they wanted to do with their days, and lived them accordingly, challenging the wind and the sea and the sun.

"Sometimes," the woman in the restaurant said, "I wish I could go back and reroute my life, and be all the people I wasn't the first time around."

She sounded braver than most of us.

"I hate myself for it," somebody said, "but I feel comfortable being safe. I'd feel happier if I could rehearse my life before having to live it. I'd like to tape the whole thing ahead of time, and edit out the rough spots." That's how most of us live our lives: editing out the rough spots by sticking to what's safe—but, ultimately, deadening.

The beauty of the *Pride of Baltimore* had nothing to do with foreign investments, and nothing to do with corporate big shots entertaining their friends on balmy nights in safe ports.

It had to do with taking chances. Most of us have quit taking chances with our lives, but the people who sailed the *Pride* did not. They were profoundly alive.

There's a character in D. H. Lawrence's *Women in Love* who says, "I don't care when I die. But when I do, I want to know that I've lived."

Most of us aren't so sure. It's easier to coast. Baltimore may have lost a goodwill ambassador when the *Pride* went down. But human beings lost something worse. We lost those who remind us what we've misplaced in our own lives: that feeling of being alive, which we never appreciate until it's too late.

MAY 22, 1986

AL SANDERS WAS HIMSELF; THAT WAS MORE THAN ENOUGH

On New Year's Eve of 1987, Al Sanders reached over and gently touched Denise Koch's arm. She squeezed his hand. Seconds later they were on the air, doing the 11 o'clock news and announcing that Jerry Turner, the legendary television anchor, was dead.

It was a remarkable broadcast, done with taste and restraint and skill while people's emotions were terribly frayed. When it was finally over, Al Sanders struggled to his feet, walked several steps off the set, and broke down sobbing. He's kept his dignity as long as he could, and now in his privacy, his defenses were all down.

The sad moment returns today, for all the worst reasons. Seven years after Turner's death from throat cancer, Al Sanders is dead from lung cancer, which was discovered too late to save him.

He was 54. He'd been urged for months to go to a hospital, but said no. He was losing too much weight, his voice had no strength, and yet cursory visits to doctors turned up nothing indicating cancer. There were fights with a friend, who finally demanded, "Why don't you go to a hospital?"

"Because of Jerry," Al admitted, choking out the words.

He was still haunted by the death of the man who'd gotten him his biggest break. Back in 1977, it was Turner who'd called a newspaper guy and declared the importance of Al Sanders. Al had been at WJZ for several years then, after coming out of St. Louis, and he had the kind of presence that convinced Turner that he was anchor quality. Management balked. Turner stood his ground.

And now, on the telephone, he said, "I want you to write something. Say you've learned that Jerry Turner wants Al Sanders as his coanchor, and if management doesn't agree, Turner's thinking of quitting and taking a job offer in California."

The newspaper column was written. The next day, the station announced Al Sanders would be coanchoring with Jerry Turner. They lasted together for the next 10 years, until Turner's death.

It is the nature of television news that it wins favor not only for its coverage of the politics and crime of the day, but also for the things viewers feel about those who broadcast it. This is very personal stuff, asking to be invited into people's living rooms every night.

In their time at WJZ-TV, Jerry Turner and Al Sanders went into more homes than the other Baltimore stations combined. They were one of the highest-rated ABC affiliates of their extended area, and there were national research figures that listed them as the top two local anchors in the country.

Al Sanders had a simple philosophy about such things, which he said Turner had passed on to him: Don't try to be somebody you're not.

"Be yourself," he counseled. "Viewers can tell when you're faking it, and they resent it."

Thus, they knew Al Sanders for more than two decades for who he really was: not only a fellow who broadcast the news, but a man who was uncommonly gentle, gracious, courtly, the most sensitive of spirits, and a deadpan comic at the right moments.

Some years back, on orders from a petty commissioner, a police intelligence unit was secretly following various public figures around town, some for the simple crime of having black skin. One of those they followed was Sanders. When confronted, the police said, "We weren't following him, we were interested in his sources."

When he heard this explanation, a thoroughly bemused Sanders declared, "I hate to say this, but I haven't got any sources."

He was being a little hard on himself. In his days as a street reporter, he approached stories with a journalist's sense of balance, and a poet's feel for language.

"You have to dream," he said one day. He was talking to a group of city school kids who didn't have much room for such things. They sat there with huge eyes, that he'd taken time to talk with them.

"I'm 50," he said that day, "and I still dream. . . . It isn't always getting what you want that makes you happiest, it's working to get something. Don't be afraid to dream. And don't be ashamed to dream."

On the night Jerry Turner died, the 11 o'clock news was almost entirely devoted to his life and death, though there was another news story, midway through the broadcast, virtually overlooked in the emotions of the evening, about a child who'd died in a fire.

In a meeting in the news director's office after the show was over, and after Al Sanders had composed his emotions, there was a sense that the program had been done professionally, that Turner himself would have approved. One voice dissented.

"I thought we handled the stuff on Jerry nicely," Al said softly. "But I think we should have done more on that kid who died in the fire."

That was Al Sanders: Everybody else saw the "other" news that night as a bother, as something merely to be waded through as a self-conscious gesture of journalistic reach, of still caring about the other business of the community. He remembered the child's death even while grieving his friend's.

So now the impossible has happened. That other towering figure in Baltimore television, Al Sanders, follows Jerry Turner to the grave. At such moments, we wish to dwell on a life well lived. We wish to imagine better times to come. We wish to think of God turning on his heavenly evening news and discovering he's got a helluva good anchor team suddenly reunited.

MAY 7, 1995

CHARLEY ECKMAN: LIVING HIS LIFE WITH THE VOLUME TURNED UP

Charley Eckman marched through life like a one-man band, all brass. The angels in heaven must be holding their ears today. Such language, Mr. Eckman! Such stories, Mr. Eckman! Oh, but, Mr. Eckman, could you tell us again about the time . . .

Which time? The time Charley refereed North Carolina and Duke in basketball, and Carolina went to its four-corner stall? It was 2–0 after 15 minutes. Everybody was yawning. Charley pulled a folding chair onto the court in the middle of play and sat himself down. "Hell," he said, "you ain't doing nothing, I ain't doing nothing."

Which time? The time he was coaching the old NBA Pistons and called time-out with seconds left in a tie game? Charley gathered his guys around him, and a moment later they scored and won. Reporters asked, "What play did you send in?" "There's only two plays," Charley said. " 'South Pacific,' and Put the Ball in the Basket."

Which time? The time he went to the old boxing promoter Eli Hanover's grandson's bris? The next morning, on his radio show, Charley declared, "First time I ever saw a clipping without a 15-yard penalty."

Yeah, those angels, they're getting an earful today, which is what the rest of us got for 72 years, until yesterday, when Charley died of cancer. It was a long and nasty fight, and late in the going he sat in his Glen Burnie home and muttered, "Everything hurts, and what doesn't hurt, doesn't work."

For a long time, though, nobody worked like Eckman. He coached the Pistons to a couple of NBA titles, and then got himself fired. He did sports on the radio for two decades and on TV for several seasons, and the only script he ever used was a couple of notes he'd jot on matchbook covers a few moments before air time.

He refereed 3,500 college basketball games over 29 seasons, and when he called a foul, it sounded like a guy taking hostages: "Nobody move," he'd bellow. "I got you right here with a hip."

"My theory," he was saying a few months back, "was, let the kids play the game. I'd talk to 'em all the time. 'Quit holding him,' I'd say. Or, 'Nice play.' You know, let 'em know I was giving 'em some room. Believe me, there's enough pressure on these kids.

"I'm refereeing at Madison Square Garden one time, and Dick McGuire's playing and he can't hit a free throw all night. There's a time out, I go over to the bench for some water, and here's this priest who goes up to McGuire. He says, 'Don't cross yourself before you make your foul shots.' McGuire says, 'Father, I've been doing it all my life.' The priest says, 'Yeah, but you missed eight in a row. You're making the religion look bad.'

"Everybody makes mistakes. When I'd call a foul, hell, I'd make it a federal case. Even if I kicked it, I made it look like I got it right. One time I made a bad call on this kid from Clemson. He says, 'What'd I do?' I said, 'Just stand there for a minute, I'll think of something.' "

He was remembering some of this over lunch one day at Sabatino's Restaurant. Somebody mentioned William Donald Schaefer. They were classmates at City College. "Did you graduate together?" somebody asked.

"Nah," Charley laughed. "Schaefer graduated before me, 'cause he copied off all the Jewish guys. I'd have done it, too, but I couldn't see that far."

Sitting a few seats from Eckman was John Vicchio, long-time roofer around town, who recalled playing a recreation league game more than half a century ago where Charley refereed and called Vicchio for a foul. Eckman remembered it. He remembered everything.

"Sure, I remember," he told Vicchio. "Your man's laying on the floor. You're going, 'I didn't hit him.' I said, 'Oh, yeah? How'd he get down there, by bus? Ain't nobody here but me and you.' "

Around the restaurant table, everybody laughed. Everybody who wasn't sitting at Charley's table waited for an empty seat at his table.

"Bring on some ugly guys," Eckman shouted. "It makes me look better."

Only occasionally did he leave clues about the needs that drove him all his life. His father died when Charley was 12. He and his mother lived in a little apartment at 1244 North Avenue. Charley remembered lying in bed at night, usually hungry, and smelling the aromas from the old Bond Bread bakery.

"One night," he remembered, "I sneak out of the house and grab a couple of buddies. I tell 'em, 'We gotta get that bread.' We're leaning in the window. We got a rope with a knife on the end, and we're gonna spear that bread right off the conveyor belt. We got three loaves when this guy comes out, yelling, 'Hey, you kids, what's going on out there?'

'We're hungry,' Eckman said.

'Well, you're honest, anyway,' the guy said, and came out with two more loaves of bread.

"Not only that," Eckman said, "but he took us to a Boy Scout meeting the next week. I walk in there with 8 cents in my pocket. These kids are all dressed up in their uniforms. He says, 'You can have one, too. For $10.95.'

"For $10.95! He might as well ask for $10 million. I couldn't pay $10 to see the pope come back. Well, what the heck, them scouts was spending all their time making knots and watching squirrels. If I tied a knot, I'm liable to hang myself."

Ironically, back in January, the Four Rivers District Boy Scouts of America gave him their Good Scout Award. Charley knew he was in bad shape, but told the crowd, "Whether I die tomorrow, it doesn't matter. I've lived. What am I gonna do, stop and wave to people, and say, 'Wait a minute, I might go'? No, you just go on living."

He lived like few of us do. Lived at fast-forward, with his volume turned full blast. Call me a cab, Charley used to say. A cab? Hell, call Charley Eckman an American original.

JULY 4, 1995

EPILOGUE

Some People Are Determined

to Stand Up for Themselves

've never bought this business about cities dying. They just go through maladies like every other living organism. Certain areas ache and rattle for a while, and then they lie dormant while restoring themselves, but just when everybody presumes them dead, they tend to rise from the grave while some other ailing area goes off to wait for a cure.

I used to stand at the rear of the *News American* and gaze at the downtown harbor directly across Pratt Street. It made me want to go home and burn all my clothes. It was an enclave of scuzzy waterfront bars and rotting warehouses and vagrant seagulls who should have moved to a better neighborhood. So, what do you know? A few people get this idea to tear it down, and they put up a thing called Harborplace, which becomes a whole city's symbol of renewal.

On Stirling Street and Barre Circle and the Otterbein neighborhood, time takes its toll on homes built nearly a century ago, making them unlivable. They're about to become ghostly. So the city sells the houses for a dollar apiece, and offers low-interest loans for rebuilding, and the nation's most famous urban homesteading program is born.

West Baltimore, drained by the parasitic narcotics traffickers, finds a sliver of life in the Sandtown-Winchester neighborhood, where government money and ordinary working people with hammers and nails reinvent a community. This, says a mayor named Schmoke to a presidential candidate named Clinton, walking him through the neighborhood, this is the thrilling part of life in an American city.

Fells Point, readied for the wrecking crews so an eight-lane highway could be built over its 18th-century buildings, its cobblestone streets, and its memories of great seafaring days, barks at the government to back off, and the government does, thus allowing the neighborhood to blossom today as a kind of funky Georgetown.

And a young community activist named Barbara Mikulski, who helped lead the fight against the highway, tells a triumphant neighborhood crowd, "The British couldn't take Fells Point, the termites couldn't take Fells Point, and the state roads commission couldn't take Fells Point."

Note the thumb-in-your-eye feistiness. It's the posture of people who feel themselves marginalized, who are determined to stand up for themselves. The city of Baltimore is changing, absolutely. But, as the 21st century dawns, with the great process of national homogenization, of McDonaldization, of computerization, the city wonders how much of its 20th-century municipal idiosyncrasies it can carry into the new day.

When I started writing news, William Donald Schaefer was enjoying the first rush of giddy and unexpected success as mayor of Baltimore. He did this by benevolently lying to everyone. The city was on its knees when he took office, still recovering from the 1968 riots a few years earlier, the public schools emptying of all children whose parents could afford private school or a home in safe suburbia, the downtown district gutted of the big department stores moving to secure, air-conditioned malls, the neighborhoods emptying of middle-class blacks and whites, the drug traffickers beginning to take over entire city blocks, the sense of dread in everyone's bones.

In the face of this, Schaefer declared, "Baltimore is Best," and built an entire public relations campaign on such farce. Immediately, everybody laughed if they didn't sneer. He seemed to be everywhere at once, always in a different funny hat. He was the city's chief cheerleader as well as chief executive. Gotta believe in ourselves, he said. Gotta think positive. He even had the town painted pink one time, and called it Pink Positive Day. It was possible, between the laughing and the sneering, to simply feel sorry for the poor deluded guy.

But a civic mindset began to change. A lot of neighborhood people who stuck around, accustomed to feeling like outsiders and unable to finance a move out of town, took him seriously. He was their last, best hope. And after a while, they seemed to be having such a good time that even the cynics wanted to sign up.

Schaefer did one thing particularly well. He surrounded himself with people like Bob Embry and Jim Rouse, Bob and Sandy Hillman and Hope Quackenbush, Walter Sondheim and Mark Joseph. They had brains and imagination. There was federal money around back then, the last vestiges of Lyndon Johnson's Great Society programs, and the city began reaching for it while it could.

Schaefer gathered a few of his people one day in 1972 and headed for an appointment with George Romney, who was Richard Nixon's secretary of Housing and Urban Development. Schaefer figured he'd pitch some projects to Romney. Romney had other ideas. He pulled out a map and began to tell Schaefer what he could have (not much) and what he couldn't (plenty). Schaefer sat there for a couple of minutes, and this terrible thought dawned on him: The fix was in. The decisions had already been made, minus any Baltimore input. Thus, he proceeded to go wild. "You don't understand what's going on in cities," he yelled at Romney. "You sit here and pretend to care. But you don't have any idea what's happening to the people affected by your decisions."

"What do you mean?" Romney said, wedging in a few words when he could. "You can't come in here and talk to me like that."

So Schaefer hollered louder. He was a crazy man. He wasn't just a mayor now, but a marginalized man, the fellow who'd lived with his mother all his life, who'd built a political career looking after alleys and pot holes and all the crap everybody else found too demeaning, who'd taken over a city because the guy before him got fed up and didn't want the job any more, and now in this room with the dignified patrician George Romney saying no to him, Schaefer decided he had nothing to lose.

"You just don't care," he yelled. The steam was practically coming out of his ears. "You don't even know what a neighborhood is." Schaefer's people, Bob Embry and Mark Joseph, sat there imagining repercussions of the worst kind. Romney's people had their eyes bugging. One of them called for a sense of perspective.

"I don't want any goddamned perspective," said Schaefer. "You all just don't care."

Romney and Schaefer both stood up. They were leaning across the table and calling each other names. The meeting was over in minutes. Everybody drove back to Baltimore thinking dark thoughts. But a wonderful thing happened in the aftermath: George Romney sat down and changed his mind on absolutely everything, and the city got money for five big development projects.

It's hard to tell precisely when it happened, but somewhere in the middle '70s, it started to become pretty hip to be from Baltimore. Maybe those first city fairs did it, when a million people from different neighborhoods gathered in the shadow of the riots to make nice to each other; maybe it was the sight of all those out-of-towners, the yuppies from Washington who suddenly wanted to buy property here, the tourists from Philly and New York who discovered Harborplace and stayed at all the big hotels springing up here; or maybe it was all those people who'd fled to the counties 10 or 15 years earlier and hadn't been back since, who suddenly looked around and couldn't believe all the people looking back at them. Maybe, a lot of them decided, there really was something to this Baltimore is Best business.

And it wasn't that visitors were overlooking our flaws, either. They saw them, and found some of them them charming. It was the antihomogenized city, complete with its own funny accents, its own ethnic festivals, and bunches of disparate people trying to get along with each other after everybody said they couldn't. At its best, it looked like America was supposed to look.

Everybody called it the Great Baltimore Renaissance, and the best of it lasted maybe a dozen years, bracketed at the dawning by the earliest City Fairs and at dusk by the coldest of rejections from Washington. The living and dying of various communities became a more precarious balancing act now. The old political warriors inevitably began to fade away. Schaefer went to Annapolis as governor, and Kurt L. Schmoke moved into City Hall, where he found problems noticeably greater than Schaefer's: In the Reagan-Bush years, Washington turned its back on cities. In Annapolis, the Washington suburban politicians, feeling new electoral muscle, tried increasingly to do the same. And, most terrifying of all, the narcotics traffickers and their criminal fallout began to get the best of it in too many places.

In the formative years of major league narcotics dealing, the early '70s, there was John "Liddie" Jones, running an $80,000-a-week drug operation, and James Wesley "Big Head Brother" Carter, who'd park his luxury car outside the Hippodrome Theatre on Eutaw Street every day to show off the television set and the bar in the back seat to all passers-by, including the cops.

They both went away to prison. The police heaved a sigh of relief, and a few imagined the worst was over. They must have been dreaming. The money was too big to be ignored, and the trafficking began to spread to dozens of operations around the city, none immediately as large as Liddie's or Big Head Brother's, but so many of them that police weren't sure where to turn first.

In the early '80s, Maurice "Peanut" King of East Baltimore took the dealing down a sinister new alley. At his peak, King headed a $50-million-a-year heroin ring, running it from an executive boardroom with computers to keep track of all the money. At North Avenue and Chester Street, he installed a fully mirrored gymnasium, two universal workout systems, punching bags, a whirlpool, plus something the cops had never seen before: a room where Peanut could adjust the weather in his little universe.

"Yeah," said the city's top narcotics cop back then, Capt. Joe Newman, "they could make it rain inside the room. They could make the wind blow. There was something called jungle mist."

And Peanut King also took the narcotics trade big-time where no one had gone before: He formed a children's brigade. He bought 18 mopeds from an East Baltimore cycle shop, and he had his lieutenants give them to school kids, some as young as 11, and then paid the kids up to $500 a week to run heroin for him. Peanut thus insulated himself from easy arrest, and the kids made a fortune. Also, the city began to be horribly afflicted by this adolescent army, swollen with unimagined money, numb to all sense of morality, disdainful of sitting through school or finding some chump job slinging hamburgers when their ship seemed to have come in. And then the kids discovered guns.

So the city enters the final years of the 20th century with mixed emotions. There's still this lovely residue left from the heady days of the renaissance, when there was money to spend and bouquets were being tossed at our feet. But we step outside our homes now, and there's a needle in the gutter, and the sound of automatic gunfire isn't so far away, and the story in the morning paper says there's been another overnight killing. A sense of combat fatigue drifts through the air.

In the public schools, they're spending textbook money to pay for security guards. They've had to close library branches, even though the mayor's words—"Baltimore: The City That Reads"—come from his heart and not from empty sloganeering. Money for literacy will have to pay for cops. When the big steel mills closed at Sparrows Point, thousands of jobs that had been secure for generations suddenly went away. The city's worked hard to create new employment, but how do you replace industries that needed massive pools of labor? Well, of course, there's that growing security field.

And always, because this is America, the issue of race stays with us.

To people who have always felt marginalized, always felt slightly cut off from the mainstream, there's the temptation to feel victimized, which is one step from feeling bitter. In tough times, such instincts are never far from the surface. In the good times here, the times when the city realized how close it had danced to the fires of hell during the riots and didn't want it to happen again, there were agreements, sometimes implicit and sometimes quite specific: We can't let race divide us. You could see it at city hall, where those like Du Burns and Mary Pat Clarke and Wally Orlinsky and Iris Reeves easily crossed color lines, and there were community groups where people worked through ancient prejudices because they had common, ad hoc goals, and later Schmoke would come along and make it clear he was evenhanded on race, he wasn't going to send the wrong kinds of signals to anyone.

But the city became an edgier place in the '90s anyway, and some of the old coalitions felt shaky. The great liberals, the Jews, moved out of Northwest Baltimore to Pikesville, and then to Owings Mills, and some to Carroll County. Little Italy was still thriving, but mostly as a village of restaurants. Many of its longtime residents found new homes in Rosedale and Timonium. In East Baltimore, the old Polish and Greek and Slovak families, for whom a big transition meant the grown kids moving to a new row house at the end of their parents' block, now looked all the way to Harford and Anne Arundel counties. And middle-class blacks who could put a few bucks together migrated by the thousands to Liberty Road in Baltimore County.

Those who have stayed in the city are thus marginalized even more: by money, by dwindling political power, by the heightened suspiciousness that accompanies any tough time. Sometimes it's not pretty. When councilmanic districts were redrawn in 1991, the council chambers filled with those drawing lines in the sand. A white city councilman took the floor to worry ominously about "the rape of neighborhoods" if a black-supported plan went through. A black councilwoman waved her shoe in the faces of white colleagues and shrieked, "The shoe is on the other foot now." It felt chilling to be there, and many wondered if the city had entered some place from which it couldn't return, or if this was just a bad cast of characters who would burn themselves out.

Because, in a thousand different places, this city can still make you feel delighted. Lexington Market still looks like America in miniature, and on balmy days you can see neighbors of every persuasion chatting on front stoops. At heart, they know there's more that unites us than divides us.

Du Burns still shows up at the Palmer House Restaurant on Eutaw Street most afternoons, talking to anybody who's in the mood about the subtleties of politics and jazz. Tom "Goose" Keyser's over at the Bay Cafe, on Boston Street in Canton, organizing trips out of town just to root *against* the Indianapolis Colts. The Baltimore Colts may have fled in 1984, but their old band is still playing, like some musical government in exile.

We plug along as best we can. Sometimes it feels like Baltimore's an old dancer who just hasn't got the legs for it any more, and sometimes we manage to rouse ourselves for a fine fandango. We keep working and working at it.

A few years back I interviewed a man named Parker Douglass, who was 103 years old and lived by himself in a house on Falls Road. He was the son of a slave. "Do you have any children?" I asked, shouting the words loud enough to penetrate his hearing aid.

"Yes," he said, "I have a son. But I don't want to talk about him. He's a bum."

"Why is he a bum?"

"He won't work."

The son was 82 years old. I like living in a place where 82-year-old men have their fathers hollering at them if they're not contributing to the life of the community. I like living in a place where a lot of people, those who feel marginalized, who feel isolated, who feel it might be tough living here but never as numbing as suburbia, work hard to keep this city's heart pumping.

LIBRARY OF CONGRESS CATALOGING-IN-PUBLICATION DATA

Olesker, Michael.
    Michael Olesker's Baltimore : if you live here, you're home /
Michael Olesker.
            p.   cm.
        ISBN 0-8018-5203-X (h : alk. paper)
        1. Baltimore (Md.) —Social life and customs.   I. Title.
F189.B15O44   1995
975.2'6—dc20   95-20454